USING THE PSSUQ AND CSUQ

in User Experience Research and Practice

James R. Lewis

ISBN-13: 978-1-7333392-0-9 (MeasuringU Press)

ISBN-10: 1-7333392-0-5

MeasuringU Press

3300 E 1st Ave Suite 300

Denver, CO 80206 USA

MeasuringU.com

Notices

Knowledge and best practices in this field constantly change. Based on new research and practical experience, it may become necessary to change research methods or professional practices. Practitioners must rely on their own experience and knowledge when using the information and methods described in this book, being mindful of their own safety and the safety of others.

To the fullest extent of the law, neither the Publisher nor the author assumes any liability for any injury and/or damage to persons or property as a matter of products liability, negligence or otherwise, or from any use or operation of any methods, products, instructions, or ideas contained in the material herein.

CONTENTS

DEDICATION

This is a book that has been over 30 years in the making, bringing together the work of many human factors engineers and user experience professionals. The initial research would never have taken place without the support of Robert Mack at the IBM T. J. Watson Research Center's User Interface Institute in the late 1980s. While I was on temporary assignment at the research center Dr. Mack gave me the opportunity to study multivariate analysis and psychometrics in the Department of Measurement and Statistics at Teacher's College, Columbia University, with Dr. Jane Monroe and Dr. Marvin Sontag. When I returned to IBM's development lab in Boca Raton, FL, my manager, Don Davis, gave me time to continue analyzing data collected at the T. J. Watson Research Center in Dr. Suzanne Henry's SUMS (System Usability Metrics) project. I am especially grateful to Dr. Mary LaLomia for her encouragement to pursue these initial analyses. More recently, I owe a strong debt of gratitude to the approximately 2000 IBM employees who are part of the IBM User Experience Panel and who have participated in surveys since 2017 to explore the relationship between the PSSUQ/CSUQ and other measures of perceived usability. Thanks also to Dr. Jeff Sauro for being a great collaborator and for his help in getting this book off the ground. And, as always, many thanks to my wonderful wife Cathy for her encouragement and support.

Welcome to *Using the PSSUQ and CSUQ in User Experience Research and Practice*. This book is for anyone who has a vested interest in assessing and improving user experiences, including UX researchers, designers, and product owners. This book draws upon my experience in the late 1980s developing the PSSUQ/CSUQ and over three decades of practical use and additional research in its psychometric properties.

Chapter 1 provides background about what the questionnaires are and where they came from.

Chapters 2 and 3 summarize research conducted on their psychometric properties.

Chapters 4 and 5 cover how to use the questionnaires in practical user research.

Chapter 6 ends the book with discussion of the future of these questionnaires and final thoughts.

Appendix A is a brief introduction to the development and assessment of standardized questionnaires.

Appendix B provides background on how to estimate sample size requirements.

The goal of this book is to provide all the information user experience practitioners need to effectively use these questionnaires, plus sufficient background in their research to justify their use to stakeholders or when crafting literature reviews for research publications.

I hope you find this book useful in your day-to-day work assessing and improving user experiences.

Finally, I want to express my gratitude for the support of Gavriel Salvendy and the *International Journal of Human-Computer Interaction* for publishing my first journal article featuring the PSSUQ and CSUQ (Lewis, 1995), and for their support in continuing to publish my PSSUQ/CSUQ-related research. Thanks also to Jeff Sauro for his comments on early drafts and providing a publication venue for this work.

James R. Lewis
Senior Human Factors Engineer
International Business Machines Corp.
drjimnfl@gmail.com

CHAPTER 1:
WHAT ARE THE PSSUQ AND CSUQ?

The Post-Study System Usability Questionnaire (PSSUQ, see Figure 1.1) and Computer System Usability Questionnaire (CSUQ, see Figure 1.2) are two widely-used questionnaires designed for the assessment of perceived usability. According to Google Scholar (6/9/2019), the original publication of the questionnaires (Lewis, 1995) has been cited over 2000 times. The questionnaires are almost identical, differing only in item wording such that the PSSUQ is appropriate for use after a standard task-based usability study and the CSUQ is appropriate for field research and for user experience surveys. The figures illustrate the latest versions of the questionnaires (Version 3). These questionnaires are in the public domain, and do not require any permission or license fee to use or modify.

SCORING RULES

PSSUQ and CSUQ ratings produce four scores:

- **Overall**: Average the responses for Items 1 through 16 (all the items)

- **System Usefulness** (SysUse): Average Items 1 through 6

- **Information Quality** (InfoQual): Average Items 7 through 12

- **Interface Quality** (IntQual): Average Items 13 through 15

The resulting scores can take values between 1 and 7, with lower scores indicating a better experience. Note that some practitioners prefer higher scores to indicate higher satisfaction, and switch the labels for "Strongly Agree" and "Strongly Disagree" (e.g., see Tullis & Albert, 2008, p. 140). From a strict interpretation of standardization, it's best to avoid this type of manipulation unless there is evidence that it does not affect the factor structure of the items.

On the other hand, the various psychometric evaluations of the PSSUQ since its initial publication suggest that it should be robust against these types of minor manipulations (Lewis, 2002). Recent research in item formats has shown that although putting the better response option on the left does not affect the magnitude of measurement, it appears to increase the number of response errors (Lewis, in press). If I were able to change one thing about these questionnaires when they were originally developed, it would be to reverse end anchors of the items. For consistency with its history and body of research, however, I will use its standard form throughout this book, as depicted in Figures 1.1 and 1.2.

When comparing across studies, it is critical to know which item format was in use and, if necessary, to adjust one of the sets of scores. To reverse a rating made on a 1-7-point scale, subtract it from 8. For example, that would change a 1 to a 7, a 7 to a 1, and would leave a 4 unchanged.

In more recent research that compares PSSUQ and CSUQ scores with the System Usability Scale (SUS, Brooke, 1996; Lewis, 2018d), I needed to convert scores to a common and consistent 0-100-point scale. As described in following chapters, this conversion enables comparison of PSSUQ and CSUQ scores with the Sauro-Lewis curved grading scale (Sauro & Lewis, 2016) – see Chapter 3 for details.

 **TIP:**

> My experience has been that practitioners can add items to the questionnaires if there is a need, or, to a limited extent, can remove items that do not make sense in a specific context. Using the PSSUQ or CSUQ as the foundation for a special-purpose questionnaire, however, ensures that practitioners can score the overall scale and subscales, maintaining the advantages of standardized measurement.

ORIGIN OF THE PSSUQ

In 1988 I was assigned to work on an IBM Research project named SUMS (System Usability MetricS, headed by Suzanne Henry), which was part of a larger research project under the direction of Robert Mack. The results of this research informed published work in usability inspection methods such as heuristic evaluation (Nielsen & Mack, 1994) and the quantification of usability (Lewis, Henry, & Mack, 1990). One of the specific tasks for the quantification of usability was to develop a standardized questionnaire to measure perceived usability.

Please indicate your level of agreement with the following statements where 1 = strongly agree (better user experience) and 7 = strongly disagree (worse user experience).

	1	2	3	4	5	6	7	NA
1. Overall, I am satisfied with how easy it is to use this system.	○	○	○	○	○	○	○	○
2. It was simple to use this system.	○	○	○	○	○	○	○	○
3. I was able to complete the tasks and scenarios quickly using this system.	○	○	○	○	○	○	○	○
4. I felt comfortable using this system.	○	○	○	○	○	○	○	○
5. It was easy to learn to use this system.	○	○	○	○	○	○	○	○
6. I believe I could become productive quickly using this system.	○	○	○	○	○	○	○	○
7. The system gave error messages that clearly told me how to fix problems.	○	○	○	○	○	○	○	○
8. Whenever I made a mistake using the system, I could recover easily and quickly.	○	○	○	○	○	○	○	○
9. The information (such as online help, on-screen messages, and other documentation) provided with this system was clear.	○	○	○	○	○	○	○	○
10. It was easy to find the information I needed.	○	○	○	○	○	○	○	○
11. The information was effective in helping me complete the tasks and scenarios.	○	○	○	○	○	○	○	○
12. The organization of information on the system screens was clear.	○	○	○	○	○	○	○	○
13. The interface of this system was pleasant. (For "interface" consider all the elements of the system's graphical user interface, which you can see, and its underlying interaction scheme, which is not necessarily visible.)	○	○	○	○	○	○	○	○
14. I liked using the interface of this system.	○	○	○	○	○	○	○	○
15. This system has all the functions and capabilities I expect it to have.	○	○	○	○	○	○	○	○
16. Overall, I am satisfied with this system.	○	○	○	○	○	○	○	○

FIGURE 1.1: The PSSUQ (Version 3).

Please indicate your level of agreement with the following statements where 1 = strongly agree (better user experience) and 7 = strongly disagree (worse user experience).

	1	2	3	4	5	6	7	NA
1. Overall, I am satisfied with how easy it is to use this system.	○	○	○	○	○	○	○	○
2. It is simple to use this system.	○	○	○	○	○	○	○	○
3. I am able to complete my work quickly using this system.	○	○	○	○	○	○	○	○
4. I feel comfortable using this system.	○	○	○	○	○	○	○	○
5. It is easy to learn to use this system.	○	○	○	○	○	○	○	○
6. I believe I became productive quickly using this system.	○	○	○	○	○	○	○	○
7. The system gives error messages that clearly tell me how to fix problems.	○	○	○	○	○	○	○	○
8. Whenever I make a mistake using the system, I recover easily and quickly.	○	○	○	○	○	○	○	○
9. The information (such as online help, on-screen messages, and other documentation) provided with this system is clear.	○	○	○	○	○	○	○	○
10. It is easy to find the information I need.	○	○	○	○	○	○	○	○
11. The information provided with the system is effective in helping me complete my work.	○	○	○	○	○	○	○	○
12. The organization of information on the system screens is clear.	○	○	○	○	○	○	○	○
13. The interface of this system is pleasant. (For 'interface' consider all the elements of the system's graphical user interface, which you can see, and its underlying interaction scheme, which is not necessarily visible.)	○	○	○	○	○	○	○	○
14. I like using the interface of this system.	○	○	○	○	○	○	○	○
15. This system has all the functions and capabilities I expect it to have.	○	○	○	○	○	○	○	○
16. Overall, I am satisfied with this system.	○	○	○	○	○	○	○	○

FIGURE 1.2: The CSUQ (Version 3).

It turned out we were not the only research group interested in developing a standardized usability questionnaire at this time. A multidisciplinary team of researchers at the Human-Computer Interaction Lab at the University of Maryland at College Park was producing the Questionnaire for User Interaction Satisfaction (QUIS – Chin, Diehl, & Norman, 1988). The first standardized questionnaire published by Human Factors Research Group at University College Cork was the Computer Usability Satisfaction Inventory (CUSI – Kirakowski & Dillon, 1988), later replaced by the Software Usability Measurement Inventory (SUMI – Kirakowski & Corbett, 1993). Although he delayed formal publication until 1996, it was around this time that John Brooke at DEC in the UK developed the System Usability Scale (SUS – Brooke, 1996, 2013). Contemporaneous with these human factors/usability research programs, Davis (1989) at the University of Michigan was conducting the information systems research that led to the Technology Acceptance Model (TAM) which demonstrated that acceptance of technology was driven by a combination of perceived usefulness and perceived ease-of-use. For a comprehensive survey of these and other standardized approaches to the measurement of usability, see Chapter 8 in *Quantifying the User Experience* (Sauro & Lewis, 2016).

We were not aware of these concurrent research efforts, however, so we conducted our own. The first version of the PSSUQ was created from a pool of items based on an early draft of the contextual usability research of Whiteside, Bennett, and Holtzblatt (1988). A group of IBM human factors engineers and usability specialists conducted content analyses of the items and recommended the inclusion of 18 items (Lewis, 1990, 1992).

A few years after the development of Version 1 of the PSSUQ, we became aware of an independent investigation at IBM into the customer perception of usability (Doug Antonelli, personal communication, January 5, 1991). This research indicated that several different user groups had identified a common set of five characteristics important to the perception of usability: quick completion of work, ease of learning, high-quality documentation and online information, rapid acquisition of productivity, and functional adequacy. The content of the 18-item version of the PSSUQ covered four of these characteristics, but did not address rapid acquisition of productivity. Version 2 included a new item added specifically to address this property of perceived usability (Lewis, 1995).

After the conclusion of the SUMS project, I continued using the PSSUQ in my research and development work at IBM. Analysis of data from five years of use indicated that three of the Version 2 items contributed very little to the reliability of the PSSUQ (Lewis, 2002), so I removed them from the PSSUQ Version 3 (Figure 1.1), the version I currently use.

ORIGIN OF THE CSUQ

In the SUMS project, 48 usability study participants completed the PSSUQ. This was a sufficient sample size for preliminary psychometric analysis, but not enough for the results to be compelling. Furthermore, the SUMS data were collected using the first version of the PSSUQ, which did not address rapid acquisition of productivity. The purpose of the CSUQ development was to create a more complete questionnaire appropriate for use as a survey rather than a questionnaire administered after a standard task-based usability study.

CHAPTER SUMMARY & TAKEAWAYS

- The PSSUQ and CSUQ are popular questionnaires for the assessment of perceived usability.

- The PSSUQ is appropriate for use at the end of standard task-based usability studies.

- The CSUQ is appropriate for field studies.

- The questionnaires produce four scores: Overall, System Usefulness, Information Quality, and Interface Quality.

- In its standard form, lower scores indicate a better user experience.

## CHAPTER 2

EARLY RESEARCH: 1988-2004

This chapter covers the research conducted to assess the psychometric quality of the PSSUQ and CSUQ during their initial development and refinement, roughly covering the time period from 1988 through 2004.

TIP:

> If you don't have a background in psychometrics, now would be a good time to read the brief review of psychometric practice in Appendix A.

PSSUQ: SUMS DATA

Method

In the SUMS project (see Chapter 1 for additional history), we conducted moderated scenario-based usability studies of three office application systems with 48 employees of temporary help agencies, evenly divided among participants with clerical/secretarial work experience and no mouse experience (this was the late 1980s), business professionals with no mouse experience, and business professionals with at least three months experience using a mouse. All participants had at least three months experience using some type of computer system, but had no programming training and limited knowledge of operating systems.

The three office application systems ran on different operating systems: Apple Macintosh (n = 15), Microsoft Windows (n = 15), and IBM Virtual Machine (n = 18). The first two were early WIMP (Windows, Icons, Menus, Pointing) systems, while the third used the local computer as a terminal to a powerful remote computer (https://en.wikipedia. org/wiki/VM_(operating_system)). All three systems allowed windowing, used a mouse as a pointing device, and allowed a certain amount of integration among the applications. The three word-processing and spreadsheet applications were similar, but the mail and calendar applications differed considerably. Participants used their assigned system to complete the following task scenarios:

- Mail (M1A): Open, reply to, and delete a note.
- Mail (M1B): Open, reply to, and delete a note.
- Mail (M2): Open a note, forward, save, and print the note.
- Address (A1): Create, change, and delete address book entries.
- File Management (F1): Rename, copy, and delete a file.
- Editor (E1): Create and save a short document.
- Editor (E2): Locate and edit a document, open a note, copy text from the note into the document, save and print the document.
- Decision Support (D1): Create a small spreadsheet, open a document, copy the spreadsheet into the document, save and print the document, and save the spreadsheet.

Participants began the study with a brief lab tour, read a description of the study's purpose and the day's agenda, and completed a background questionnaire. They spent their first hour learning how to use a WIMP system, specifically moving pointing and selecting with a mouse, opening icons, and maximizing and minimizing windows. Next they worked on the scenarios. While participants performed scenarios, observers logged the activities. If the participant completed a scenario without assistance and produced the correct output, the observer recorded that scenario as successfully completed. At the end of each scenario participants completed the After-Scenario Questionnaire (ASQ, Lewis, 1995; Sauro & Lewis, 2016), a short questionnaire with items for satisfaction with the ease and speed of task completion, plus satisfaction with supporting information. After finishing their work on the scenarios (either having worked on all scenarios or finishing the 8-hour work day), completed the original 18-item version of the PSSUQ (see Figure 2.1).

Please indicate your level of agreement with the following statements where 1 = strongly agree (better user experience) and 7 = strongly disagree (worse user experience).

	1	2	3	4	5	6	7	NA
1. Overall, I am satisfied with how easy it is to use this system.	○	○	○	○	○	○	○	○
2. It was simple to use this system.	○	○	○	○	○	○	○	○
3. I could effectively complete the tasks and scenarios using this system.	○	○	○	○	○	○	○	○
4. I was able to complete the tasks and scenarios quickly using this system.	○	○	○	○	○	○	○	○
5. I was able to efficiently complete the tasks and scenarios using this system.	○	○	○	○	○	○	○	○
6. I felt comfortable using this system.	○	○	○	○	○	○	○	○
7. It was easy to learn to use this system.	○	○	○	○	○	○	○	○
8. The system gave error messages that clearly told me how to fix problems.	○	○	○	○	○	○	○	○
9. Whenever I made a mistake using the system, I could recover easily and quickly.	○	○	○	○	○	○	○	○
10. The information (such as online help, on-screen messages, and other documentation) provided with this system was clear.	○	○	○	○	○	○	○	○
11. It was easy to find the information I needed.	○	○	○	○	○	○	○	○
12. The information provided for the system was easy to understand.	○	○	○	○	○	○	○	○
13. The information was effective in helping me complete the tasks and scenarios.	○	○	○	○	○	○	○	○
14. The organization of information on the system screens was clear.	○	○	○	○	○	○	○	○
15. The interface of this system was pleasant. (Note: The interface includes those items that you use to interact with the system. For example, some components of the interface are the keyboard, the mouse, and the screens, including their use of graphics and language.)	○	○	○	○	○	○	○	○
16. I liked using the interface of this system.	○	○	○	○	○	○	○	○
17. This system has all the functions and capabilities I expect it to have.	○	○	○	○	○	○	○	○
18. Overall, I am satisfied with this system.	○	○	○	○	○	○	○	○

FIGURE 2.1: The PSSUQ (Version 1).

Participants received the following instructions for completing the PSSUQ:

This questionnaire gives you an opportunity to tell us your reactions to the system you used. Your responses will help us understand what aspects of the system you are particularly concerned about and the aspects that satisfy you. To as great a degree as possible, think about all the tasks that you have done with the system while you answer these questions. Please read each statement and indicate how strongly you agree or disagree with the statement by selecting a number on the scale. If a statement does not apply to you, select NA. Please write comments to elaborate on your answers. After you have completed this questionnaire, I'll go over your answers with you to make sure I understand all of your responses. Thank you!

Results

A common rule-of-thumb for the sample size for factor analysis is five participants per item (Nunnally, 1978), which, for 18 items, would be 90 participants. There were only 48 participants in the SUMS study, however, so these results were considered preliminary.

Number of Factors

The first step was to conduct an exploratory principal factor analysis for the purpose of identifying (1) the number of factors and (2) which items were most strongly associated with the factors. Discontinuity analysis (Coovert & McNelis, 1988) indicated that three factors were appropriate (see Figure 2.2).

Discontinuity analysis examines the differences between the sequence of eigenvalues computed for each possible factor which equals the number of items (Cliff, 1987). In Figure 2.2, negative eigenvalues were assigned the value of 0. The justification for a three-factor solution was the observation that the difference between the third and fourth eigenvalues was greater than the difference between the second and third eigenvalues – in other words, a discontinuity. Additional eigenvalue analysis indicated that the three factors accounted for 87% of the variability in the data.

 **TIP:**

> "Eigenvalue" is a term from matrix algebra which is used in factor analysis. For the purpose of this analysis it isn't necessary to understand how to compute eigenvalues; it's just necessary to know that they are used in various ways to estimate the appropriate number of factors.

Item Analysis

Table 2.1 shows the varimax-rotated factor loadings for the three-factor solution. With a few exceptions, items more strongly aligned with one factor than the others. The exceptions were Item 14 (strong loadings on Factors 2 and 3) and 18 (strong loadings on Factors 1 and 3). Due to their ambiguous alignment, they were not assigned to a factor when naming the factors.

Naming Subscales

Like most statistical analysis, factor analysis is a blend of mathematics and human judgment. Naming factors is part of the art of exploratory factor analysis. Based on the item content of each factor, a group of human factors engineers and usability specialists named the factors (and their corresponding subscales) System Usefulness (SysUse), Information Quality (InfoQual), and Interface Quality (IntQual).

Item	Factor 1	Factor 2	Factor 3
1	**0.77**	0.26	0.43
2	**0.63**	0.35	0.46
3	**0.75**	0.38	0.25
4	**0.81**	0.45	0.07
5	**0.80**	0.16	0.36
6	**0.68**	0.37	0.48
7	**0.69**	0.46	0.40
8	0.05	**0.61**	0.24
9	0.36	**0.71**	0.23
10	0.45	**0.63**	0.25
11	0.44	**0.75**	0.22
12	0.43	**0.70**	0.32
13	0.43	**0.74**	0.40
14	0.30	**0.59**	**0.56**
15	0.30	0.36	**0.75**
16	0.37	0.36	**0.76**
17	0.22	0.28	**0.80**
18	**0.58**	0.21	**0.64**

TABLE 2.1: Item loadings for SUMS participants' responses to the PSSUQ Version 1.

Scale Reliability

Reliability analyses using coefficient alpha showed that the reliability of the overall summative scale (Overall) was 0.97, with acceptable subscale reliabilities (SysUse: 0.96, InfoQual: 0.91, IntQual: 0.91). All reliabilities were substantially higher than the minimum goal of 0.70 (Nunnally, 1978).

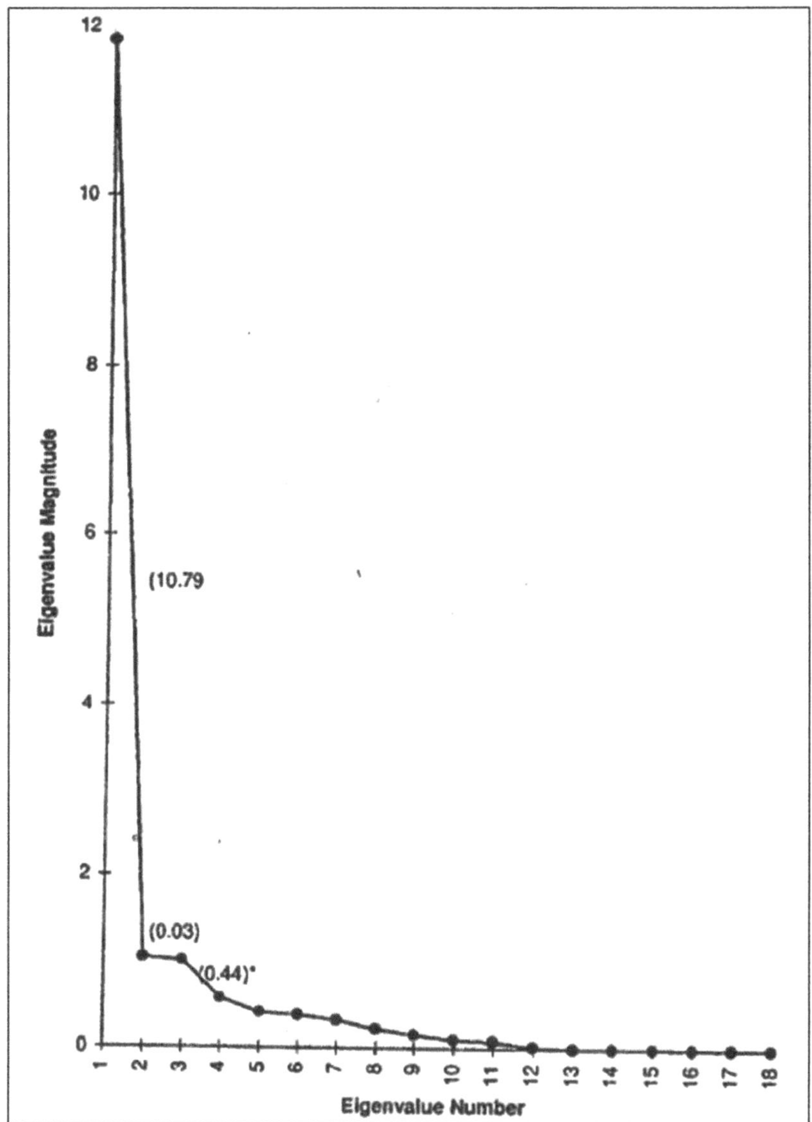

FIGURE 2.2: Discontinuity analysis of SUMS participants' responses to the PSSUQ Version 1.

Concurrent Validity

A subset of participants completed all PSSUQ and ASQ items and attempted all eight scenarios, permitting correlation analyses among perceived usability (both overall and at the task level) and successful task completion rates. The overall PSSUQ scores correlated highly with the sum of ASQ scores across the scenarios ($r(20) = 0.80$, $p < 0.0001$). The overall PSSUQ scores also correlated significantly with the percentage of successful scenario completions ($r(29) = -0.40$, $p = 0.026$). There was a highly significant correlation between SysUse and successful scenario completions ($r(36) = -0.40$, $p = 0.006$). The correlation between IntQual and successful scenario completions was relatively strong ($r(35) = -0.29$, $p = 0.08$), but not quite statistically significant using the typical criterion of $p < 0.05$ (but see Sauro & Lewis, 2016, Chapter 9, "Can you reject the null hypothesis when $p > 0.05$?").

Calculating Scale Scores

In classical psychometric theory (Nunnally, 1978), the usual method for calculating the score for a summative scale is to add the ratings. For the PSSUQ, however, we decided to take the average of the scores. From a statistical perspective (e.g., correlations and tests of significance) this type of linear manipulation has no effect on outcomes. Averaging items to obtain scale scores standardizes the range of scale scores, making them easier to interpret and compare when scales are made up of different numbers of items. Another advantage of averaging is that if an item is not appropriate in a specific context and users choose not to answer it, the questionnaire is still useful because users who do not answer every item can stay in the sample.

This method of calculating scale scores gives equal weight to each item in the scale. Although it is a standard practice to weight items equally, one consequence of this is that the resulting scales will correlate to some extent rather than being independent. As Nunnally (1978, p. 434) wrote, "Although the factors themselves are uncorrelated, this does not mean that estimated factor scores are uncorrelated … Usually they are only estimated, not obtained directly, … In these cases the estimated factor scores are likely to correlate substantially even if the factors themselves are orthogonal." This is usually not a problem as long as (a) the correlations are not too close to 1.0 (avoiding multicollinearity) and (b) the scales are useful in interpreting measurement outcomes.

Sensitivity

Analyses of variance (ANOVAs) were conducted for Overall and each subscale using data from 38 SUMS participants. The ANOVAs assessed main effects of System (three levels based on the system used to attempt the scenarios) and Group (three levels based on the type of participant – clerical worker without mouse experience, business professional without mouse experience, business professional with mouse experience), and their interaction. For all four dependent variables, there were significant main effects of Group (Overall: $F(2, 29) = 4.35$, $p = 0.02$; SysUse: $F(2, 36) = 6.9$, $p = 0.003$; InfoQual: $F(2, 33) = 3.68$, $p = 0.04$); IntQual: $F(2, 35) = 3.74$, $p = 0.03$). The only significant main effect for System was for InfoQual ($F(2, 33) = 3.18$, $p = 0.05$). There were no significant Group by System interactions.

A multivariate analysis of variance (MANOVA) using SysUse, InfoQual, and IntQual as dependent measures for generalized F tests (F_0: see Cliff, 1987) detected significant differences among systems ($F_0(2, 2, 28) = 11.53$, $p < 0.01$), marginally significant differences among groups ($F_0(2, 2, 28) = 5.74$, $p < 0.10$, but no System by Group interaction.

Discussion

Due to the small sample size, although promising, these findings were preliminary. The exploratory factor analysis and reliability analyses suggested that it would be reasonable to define three PSSUQ subscales: SysUse, InfoQual, and IntQual. The PSSUQ demonstrated reasonable concurrent validity through its correlations with successful completion rates and ASQ scores. The evidence provided sufficient justification to move to a second phase of research using the CSUQ to collect more data in a different research context to extend the generalizability of the findings.

CSUQ: FIRST SURVEY

Method

Before I conducted the first survey with the CSUQ, I had added the 19th item to the second version of the PSSUQ (see Chapter 1). To investigate the psychometric properties of these items in a different research context with a larger sample size, I revised the wording of the items as shown in Figure 2.3, then sent the questionnaire to 825 randomly selected IBM employees at nine different development sites. Participants received a paper copy of the CSUQ with a cover letter asking them to use it to rate their satisfaction with their primary computer system. I waited three months to begin data analysis, receiving 377 completed questionnaires in that time. The instructions sent with the questionnaire were:

This questionnaire gives you an opportunity to express your satisfaction with the usability of your primary computer system. Your responses will help us understand what aspects of the system you are particularly concerned about and the aspects that satisfy you. To as great a degree as possible, think about all the tasks that you have done with the system while you answer these questions. Please read each statement and indicate how strongly you agree or disagree with the statement by selecting a number on the scale. If a statement does not apply to you, select NA. Whenever it is appropriate, please write comments to explain your answers. Thank you!

Results

Number of Factors

Discontinuity analysis of the eigenvalues from both principal factor analysis and maximum likelihood factor analysis indicated retention of three factors, with scree plots similar to that shown in Figure 2.2. The three factors accounted for 98.6% of the variability in the rating data.

Item Analysis

Table 2.2 shows the varimax-rotated factor loadings for the principal factor analysis. The new Item 8 (I believe I became productive quickly using this system") aligned with the first factor (SysUse). Item 15 ("The organization of information on the system screens is clear"), which loaded on two factors in the first PSSUQ study, loaded only on Factor 2 (InfoQual) in the current study. Once again, the last item (Item 19 in Version 2, "Overall, I am satisfied with this system") loaded on both Factors 1 and 3, so it was not assigned to a subscale although it was still part of the overall scale. Otherwise, the factor structure of the CSUQ was very similar to that of the PSSUQ, so the CSUQ subscales have the same names as those used for the PSSUQ.

Scale Reliability

For the overall scale and the three subscales, all coefficient alphas exceeded 0.89, indicating acceptable scale reliability. The estimates of coefficient alpha for the CSUQ were 0.93 for SysUse, 0.91 for InfoQual, 0.89 for IntQual, and 0.95 for Overall. The values of coefficient alpha for the CSUQ scales were within 0.03 of those for the PSSUQ scales.

Sensitivity

Because there were no concurrently collected measures of objective or perceived usability with the survey methodology, it was not possible to obtain quantitative measures of concurrent validity. An indirect way to assess validity is to examine scale sensitivity to variables that could systematically affect scale scores. The previous sensitivity analyses of the PSSUQ showed significant effects of user group on Overall, SysUse, InfoQual, and IntQual. The type of computer system the participant used significantly affected InfoQual.

Please indicate your level of agreement with the following statements where 1 = strongly agree (better user experience) and 7 = strongly disagree (worse user experience).	1	2	3	4	5	6	7	NA
1. Overall, I am satisfied with how easy it is to use this system.	O	O	O	O	O	O	O	O
2. It is simple to use this system.	O	O	O	O	O	O	O	O
3. I can effectively complete my work using this system.	O	O	O	O	O	O	O	O
4. I am able to complete my work quickly using this system.	O	O	O	O	O	O	O	O
5. I am able to efficiently complete my work using this system.	O	O	O	O	O	O	O	O
6. I feel comfortable using this system.	O	O	O	O	O	O	O	O
7. It was easy to learn to use this system.	O	O	O	O	O	O	O	O
8. I believe I became productive quickly using this system.	O	O	O	O	O	O	O	O
9. The system gives error messages that clearly tell me how to fix problems.	O	O	O	O	O	O	O	O
10. Whenever I make a mistake using the system, I recover easily and quickly.	O	O	O	O	O	O	O	O
11. The information (such as online help, on-screen messages, and other documentation) provided with this system is clear.	O	O	O	O	O	O	O	O
12. It is easy to find the information I need.	O	O	O	O	O	O	O	O
13. The information provided with the system is easy to understand.	O	O	O	O	O	O	O	O
14. The information is effective in helping me complete my work.	O	O	O	O	O	O	O	O
15. The organization of information on the system screens is clear.	O	O	O	O	O	O	O	O
16. The interface of this system is pleasant. (Note: The interface includes those items that you use to interact with the system. For example, some components of the interface are the keyboard, the mouse, and the screens, including their use of graphics and language.)	O	O	O	O	O	O	O	O
17. I like using the interface of this system.	O	O	O	O	O	O	O	O
18. This system has all the functions and capabilities I expect it to have.	O	O	O	O	O	O	O	O
19. Overall, I am satisfied with this system.	O	O	O	O	O	O	O	O

FIGURE 2.3: The CSUQ (Version 2).

Significant findings with the CSUQ were similar to those for the preliminary investigation of the PSSUQ. The type of computer that respondents used marginally affected their response for InfoQual ($F(5, 311) = 2.14$, $p = 0.06$). The number of years of experience with the system significantly affected Overall ($F(5, 294) = 3.12$, $p = 0.02$), InfoQual ($F(4, 311) = 2.59$, $p = 0.04$), and IntQual ($F(4, 322) = 2.47$, $p = 0.04$), and marginally affected SysUse (F(4, 332) = 2.05, p = 0.09). The respondents' range of experience with computer systems (number of different computer systems that they reported having used) significantly affected scores for Overall (F(3, 294) = 2.77, p = 0.04) and InfoQual (F(3, 311) = 2.60, p = 0.05), and marginally affected IntQual (F(3, 322) = 2.14, p = 0.10). These findings provided indirect support of scale validity. As with the previous PSSUQ analyses, the error degrees of freedom in the F-tests varied according to the number of participants who completed all the items on the given scale and on the associated demographics questions.

Item	SysUse	InfoQual	IntQual
1	**0.74**	0.36	0.26
2	**0.69**	0.41	0.16
3	**0.72**	0.21	0.36
4	**0.74**	0.31	0.33
5	**0.77**	0.30	0.32
6	**0.72**	0.22	0.27
7	**0.63**	0.49	0.13
8	**0.66**	0.39	0.26
9	0.23	**0.72**	0.21
10	0.34	**0.67**	0.28
11	0.23	**0.81**	0.20
12	0.24	**0.77**	0.27
13	0.38	**0.76**	0.17
14	0.40	**0.73**	0.18
15	0.34	**0.57**	0.40
16	0.33	0.27	**0.81**
17	0.38	0.26	**0.81**
18	0.34	0.35	**0.56**
19	**0.66**	0.37	**0.50**

TABLE 2.2: Item loadings for respondent's ratings with the CSUQ Version 2.

Discussion

The key results from this survey study were (a) a demonstration of a reasonably stable factor structure for these items and (b) evidence that the questionnaire worked well in a non-laboratory setting. The CSUQ scales were comparable to the PSSUQ scales, both in terms of reliability and validity (indicated by the similarities in the sensitivity analyses). This consistency provided strong evidence of generalizability of results and potentially wide applicability of the questionnaires (PSSUQ for lab studies; CSUQ for surveys or field studies).

REVISITING THE PSSUQ WITH FIVE YEARS OF USABILITY TESTING DATA

In 2001, usability researchers and practitioners from IBM were invited to submit papers for a special issue of the International Journal of Human-Computer Interaction (Lewis, 2002). At that time, I had been using the PSSUQ (Version 2) regularly for about five years, primarily for usability studies of speech recognition systems with a focus on dictation.

Replication of Psychometric Findings

For this study, the primary research question was whether the PSSUQ, used for research in a new context, would have structure, reliability, validity, and sensitivity consistent with its previous research. Replication of the previous findings with this new set of data would provide additional evidence of generalizability for the questionnaire, supporting its use by practitioners for the measurement of perceived usability.

Control of Potential Response Style or Consistency in Item Alignment

Another goal of the research was to investigate potential effects of response style on PSSUQ scores. It is a common practice in questionnaire development to vary the tone of items so, typically, one half of the items elicit agreement and the other half elicit disagreement. The purpose of this practice is to control potential measurement bias due to a respondent's response style. An alternative approach is to align the items consistently with a positive tone.

A potential criticism of the PSSUQ and CSUQ was that we did not use the standard approach to control for potential measurement bias due to response style (Travis, 2008), instead aligning the items consistently with a positive tone. Our rationale was to make it as easy as possible for participants to complete the questionnaire. With consistent item alignment, the proper way to mark responses on the scales is clearer and requires less interpretive effort on the part of the participant, potentially reducing response errors due to participant confusion (an approach later supported by experimentation with different versions of the SUS – see Sauro & Lewis, 2011).

Furthermore, the use of negatively worded items can produce a number of undesirable effects (Ibrahim, 2001), including "problems with internal consistency, factor structures, and other statistics when negatively worded items are used either along or together with directly worded stems" (Barnette, 2000, p. 363). This led Barnette to recommend, "Unless there is some pervasive and unambiguous reason for not doing so, it is probably best that all items be positively or directly worded and not mixed with negatively worded items" (p. 363).

Nunnally (1978, pp. 658-672) provided a review of the various types of response styles. The major types of styles that have been hypothesized to exist are social desirability, the tendency to guess when in doubt, the tendency to guess "true," the acquiescence (agreement) tendency, the extreme response tendency, and the deviant response tendency. Most of these do not logically apply to usability assessment settings, but acquiescence and extreme response tendencies, if present, could affect PSSUQ and CSUQ scores. Unfortunately, there is no empirical test to run on a set of usability questionnaire responses to determine the presence of acquiescence, but for the most part, research both before (Nunnally, 1978) and after (Sauro & Lewis, 2011) this study has shown, as Nunnally stated, "the overwhelming weight of the evidence now points to the fact that the acquiescence tendency is of very little importance either as a measure of personality or as a source of systematic invalidity in measures of personality and sentiments" (p. 669). It is possible with a single set of questionnaire data to investigate the likely presence or absence of the extreme response tendency (Nunnally, 1978).

Preliminary Norms

The scores of standardized usability questionnaires are always useful when comparing two sets of scores, but without norms it isn't possible to interpret whether a given individual mean is consistent with a poor or good user experience. Another goal of this research was to create preliminary sets of norms for the PSSUQ and CSUQ and to inspect them for useful normative patterns.

Method

The data analyzed in this study came from 21 unpublished usability studies conducted in our lab, during which participants completed the PSSUQ (Version 2, paper-and-pencil administration) at the end of the study. Most of the studies (90%) were investigations of speech recognition systems, both IBM and non-IBM, with an emphasis on speech dictation. The other studies were of an early version of a smart phone (the Simon, see Lewis, 1996;   https://www.wallstreetdaily.com/2014/08/16/ibm-simon-smart-phone/) and a handwriting/sketching capture device (the CrossPad, see Lewis, 2004; https://www.industryweek.com/information-technology/cross-pen-computing-group-div-cross-colincoln-ri).

The PSSUQ database created from these questionnaires had 210 cases from participants of widely varying backgrounds. With this database, it was possible to investigate the effect of the following independent variables on the profile of the PSSUQ scales: Study, Developer, Stage of Development, Type of Product, Type of Evaluation, Gender, and Completeness of Response. See the Sensitivity section in the Results for more detailed descriptions of these independent variables and the outcomes of their evaluation.

Results

Factor Analysis

As in the initial PSSUQ and CSUQ evaluations, a discontinuity analysis indicated a three-factor solution (note the increase in the difference between the third and fourth eigenvalues in Figure 2.4 relative to the difference between the second and third. Table 2.3 shows the item loadings for the varimax-rotated three-factor solution, which explained 72.5% of the variance in the data.

This factor structure was very similar to the structures found for the initial PSSUQ and CSUQ studies described at the beginning of this chapter, but there were some minor differences. In this analysis, the 19th item loaded strongly on the first factor (SysUse) whereas in the past it loaded about equally on the first and third factors (SysUse and IntQual). Items 7 and 10 loaded about equally on the first and second factors (SysUse and InfoQual), and Item 15 loaded about equally on the second and third factors (InfoQual and IntQual). In the previous evaluations, Item 7 loaded most strongly on SysUse, and Items 10 and 15 loaded most strongly on InfoQual. For continuity with previous research and pending future research on item loading, I resolved ambiguities in favor of the existing PSSUQ scale definitions (SysUse: 1-8, InfoQual: 9-15, IntQual: 16-18, Overall: 1-19) when conducting reliability and sensitivity analyses.

As expected (Nunnally, 1978), an analysis of the correlations among the estimated factor scores showed substantial correlation: SysUse-InfoQual, $r(203) = 0.72$; SysUse-IntQual, $r(207) = 0.67$; InfoQual-IntQual, $r(203) = 0.56$; all $p < 0.000002$. In the initial PSSUQ study, the same pairs of estimated factor scores had correlations of 0.71, 0.68, and 0.64, and in the initial CSUQ study were 0.67, 0.71, and 0.61. Therefore, across the studies up to this time, the intercorrelations appeared to be about 0.7, 0.7, and 0.6, so the estimated factor scores shared about 36-50% of their variance. Although these correlations were significantly different from zero, they were not so close to one another that they would cause multicollinearity problems during statistical analysis.

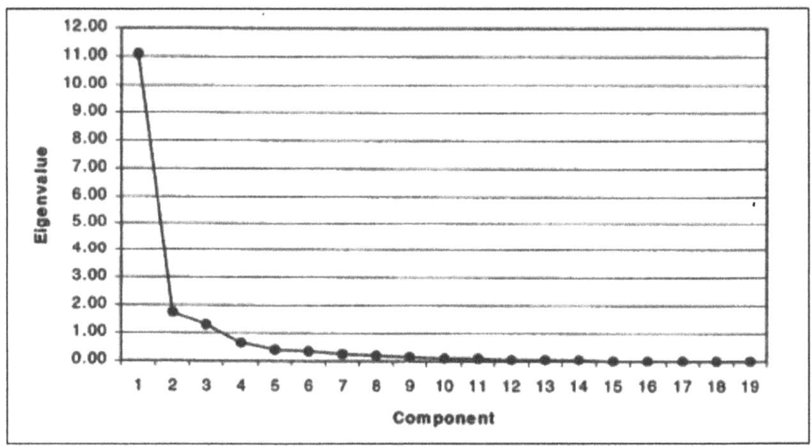

FIGURE 2.4: Discontinuity analysis of participants' responses to the PSSUQ Version 2.

Scale Reliability

Estimates of reliability using coefficient alpha indicated levels of reliability for the overall PSSUQ and its factor-based subscales that were consistent with previous estimates: Overall: 0.96, SysUse: 0.96, InfoQual: 0.92, IntQual: 0.83. Because it is possible to obtain high reliabilities for a scale by including multiple items that mean exactly the same (either worded in the same or a similar way), some critics of the PSSUQ had suggested that this could be the basis for its highly reliable scales. Specifically, they had noted the similarity among Item 3 (effective task completion), Item 4 (quick task completion), and Item 5 (efficient task completion) in SysUse; and between Item 11 (clear information) and Item 13 (information easy to understand) in InfoQual.

To investigate the possibility that the high reliability for the PSSUQ scales was due to these highly similar items, I recalculated the reliabilities for SysUse without Items 3 and 5, InfoQual without Item 13, and the revised Overall scale without these items. Without Items 3 and 5, the reliability of SysUse fell from 0.96 to 0.90 – still very high. InfoQual declined slightly from 0.93 to 0.91, and the effect on Overall was to reduce coefficient alpha from 0.96 to 0.94 – a negligible reduction.

The correlation between the original scores and the revised scores was 0.99 for SysUse, 1.00 for InfoQual, and 1.00 for Overall. The differences between the mean scores for the original and revised versions of these scales (with 99% confidence intervals) were 0.05 ± 0.02, -0.06 ± 0.02, and 0.01 ± 0.01, respectively. The SysUse mean shifted up slightly (somewhere between 0.03 and 0.07 and the InfoQual mean shifted down slightly (somewhere between -0.04 and -0.08), for both measurements less than one tenth of a scale step. The net effect was that the Overall score essentially did not change (somewhere between 0 and 0.02 – less than one fiftieth of a scale step).

Item	SysUse	InfoQual	IntQual
1	**0.83**	0.38	0.23
2	**0.62**	0.46	0.20
3	**0.79**	0.35	0.17
4	**0.82**	0.25	0.22
5	**0.82**	0.26	0.32
6	**0.73**	0.40	0.20
7	**0.47**	**0.45**	0.38
8	**0.73**	0.19	0.29
9	0.32	**0.60**	0.13
10	**0.59**	**0.56**	0.14
11	0.24	**0.89**	0.21
12	0.28	**0.83**	0.15
13	0.32	**0.81**	0.13
14	0.36	**0.79**	0.21
15	0.15	**0.51**	**0.47**
16	0.20	0.19	**0.86**
17	0.36	0.10	**0.86**
18	0.38	0.27	**0.54**
19	**0.76**	0.27	0.37

TABLE 2.3: Item loadings for respondent's ratings with the PSSUQ Version 2.

Sensitivity

The Overall PSSUQ score was 2.8, with means of 2.8 for SysUse, 3.0 for InfoQual, and 2.5 for IntQual. Remember that for the standard PSSUQ, lower scores indicate a better user experience. Analyses of variance conducted to investigate the sensitivity of PSSUQ measures indicated that the following variables significantly affected PSSUQ scores, as indicated by a main effect, an interaction with the three PSSUQ subscales, or both:

- Study (21 levels – the study during which participants completed the PSSUQ)
- Developer (4 levels – the company that developed the product under evaluation)
- Stage of development (2 levels – product under development or available for purchase)
- Type of product (5 levels – discrete dictation, continuous dictation, game, personal communicator, or pen product)
- Type of evaluation (2 levels – dictation study or standard usability evaluation)

The following variables did not significantly affect PSSUQ scores:

- Gender (2 levels – male or female)
- Completeness of responses to questionnaire (2 levels – complete or incomplete)

Study

Both the main effect, $F(20, 184) = 2.2$, $p = 0.004$, and the interaction, $F(40, 368) = 3.2$, $p = 0.000000003$ (see Figure 2.5) were significant; overall means across the 21 studies (labeled using the letters A through U for reasons of confidentiality) ranged from 1.9 to 4.2. Note that (a) none of the lines were horizontal and (b) the magnitude of differences among SysUse, InfoQual, and IntQual varied across the studies (in other words, the lines were not parallel)—patterns that indicate scale sensitivity.

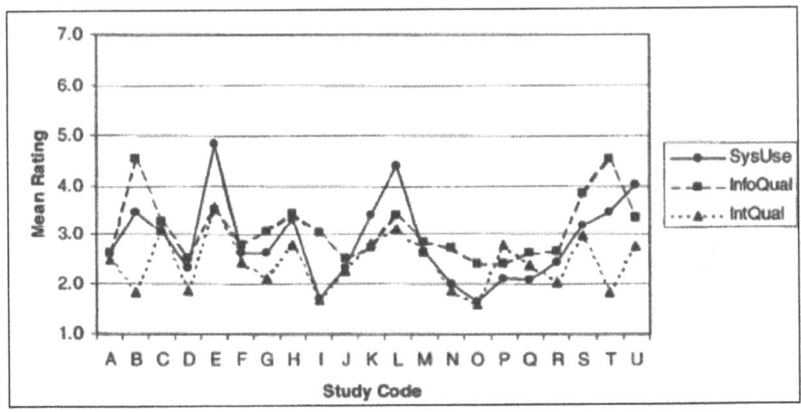

FIGURE 2.5: Study by subscale interaction.

Developer

This variable refers to the company that developed the product under study (with companies coded as CIC, CDC, CKC, and CMC for reasons of confidentiality). Both the main effect, $F(3, 201) = 3.4$, $p = 0.02$, and the interaction, $F(6, 402) = 3.6$, $p = 0.002$ were significant; overall means across developers ranged from 2.5 to 3.3. The pattern of results were similar to those for Study in that (a) none of the lines were horizontal and (b) the magnitude of differences among SysUse, InfoQual, and IntQual varied across developers—overall patterns indicative of scale sensitivity.

Stage of Development

This variable refers to whether the investigated product was in development or available for purchase. Both the main effect ($F(1, 203) = 4.2$, $p = 0.04$, and the interaction ($F(2, 206) = 3.1$, $p = 0.05$ (see Figure 2.6) were significant. Products under development received better ratings than products available for purchase (overall means of 2.6 and 3.0, respectively). The pattern of the interaction (assessed using Bonferroni t tests with ▯ $= 0.017$) was that mean ratings of IntQual differed by 0.2 (development, 2.4; product, $2.6 - t(207) = 1.1$, $p = 0.28$), ratings of InfoQual differed by 0.3 (development, 2.9; product, $3.2 - t(207) = 1.7$, $p = 0.08$), and ratings of SysUse differed by 0.5 (development, 2.6; product, $3.1 - t(207) = 3.1$, $p = 0.002$).

This outcome was a somewhat surprising result that might be due to a number of factors. For example, when evaluating a product under development, the range of tasks that the product can perform is more limited than will be the case once the product is complete. This limited functionality affects the number (and possibly the complexity) of tasks that an evaluator can ask participants to perform with the product (which is consistent with the significant difference for SysUse).

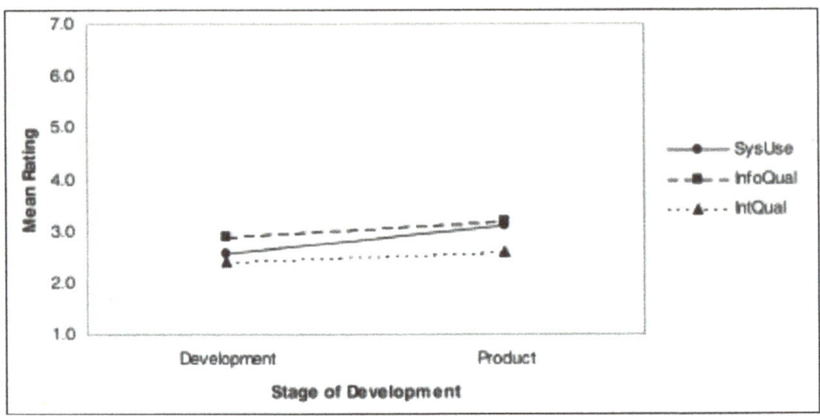

FIGURE 2.6: Stage of development by subscale interaction.

Type of Product

This variable refers to the type of product under investigation. The types of products included:

- Continuous dictation products: Products that allow users to speak continuously when dictating text

- Discrete dictation products: Products that require users to briefly pause between words when dictating

- Speech control of computer games: Product that allowed users to control computer games by issuing voice commands

- Personal communicator: A combination cellular phone and personal digital assistant device

- Pen computing device: A device for capturing and managing handwritten notes

The main effect, $F(4, 200) = 1.9$, $p = 0.11$, was not significant; but the interaction, $F(8, 400) = 2.3$, $p = 0.02$, was (see Figure 2.7). As was the case for the variables of Study and Developer, (a) the lines were not horizontal and (b) differences among the scales were not identical across developers – patterns that provide evidence of sensitivity to the product type.

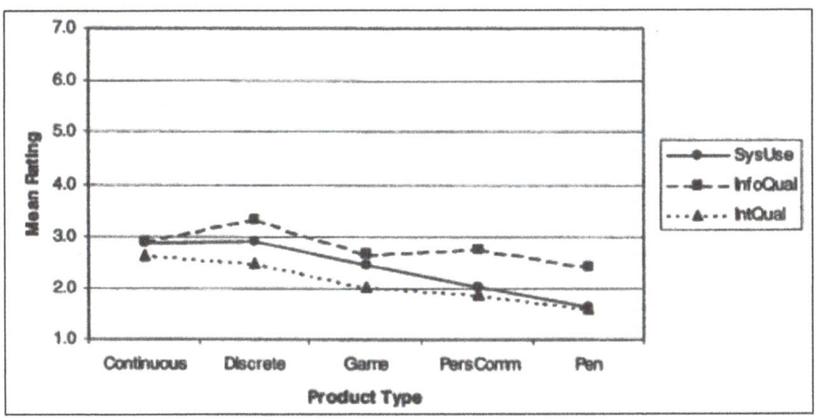

FIGURE 2.7: Product type by subscale interaction.

Type of Evaluation

This variable refers to the type of evaluation conducted in the study: dictation and standard. "Dictation" refers to the use of a specific protocol we developed for the measurement of dictation speed and accuracy (Lewis, 1999). The task in the dictation studies was for a user to dictate from written source text and, in some studies, to also use the system to compose documents. In most dictation studies, participants received training in how to dictate and correct, and rarely consulted any system documentation.

"Standard" refers to the use of a standard scenario-based usability problem discovery protocol (e.g., see Lewis et al., 1990). In this protocol, the typical procedure was for participants to receive descriptions of tasks to complete with the system under evaluation. In most cases, the tasks were organized within scenarios designed to provide broad functional coverage. In most standard evaluations, participants had access to system documentation and used it as required.

The main effect, $F(1, 203) = 0.004$, $p = 0.99$, was not significant; but the interaction, $F(2, 406) = 7.6$, $p = 0.001$, was (see Figure 2.8). Post hoc examination of the interaction using Bonferroni t tests (with $\alpha = 0.008$) indicated that for dictation studies, SysUse and InfoQual were not significantly different from one another, $t(123) = 0.6$, $p = 0.54$; but both were significantly different from IntQual, $t(127) = 4.2$, $p = 0.0001$, and $t(123) = 4.8$, $p = 0.000005$, respectively. For dictation studies, SysUse and IntQual were not dramatically different from one another, $t(80) = 1.95$, $p = 0.055$; but both were significantly different from InfoQual, $t(80) = 5.9$, $p = 0.0000001$, and $t(80) = 5.28$, $p = 0.000001$, respectively.

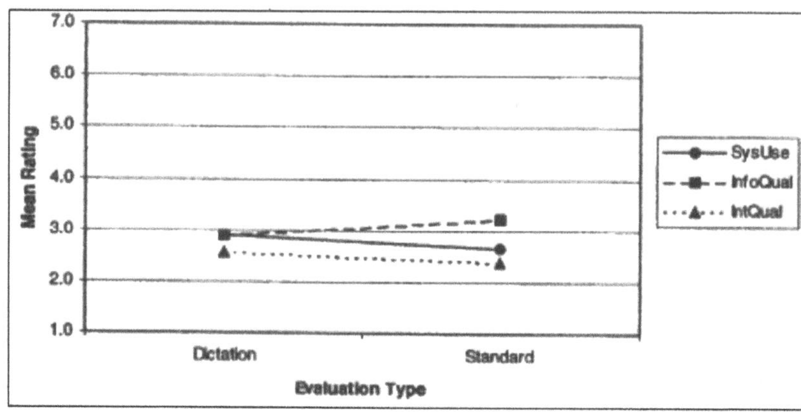

FIGURE 2.8: Evaluation type by subscale interaction.

Keeping in mind that these data are not from a designed experiment, it seems reasonable that the difference in the use of system documentation between the evaluation methods (not used in dictation studies, used in standard studies) could account for the difference in the PSSUQ scale patterns. Therefore, these results do not only indicate scale sensitivity by virtue of a significant interaction, but also by virtue of the different behavior of InfoQual as a function of the type of study.

Gender

Neither the main effect, $F(1, 194) = 0.12$, $p = 0.74$, nor the interaction, $F(2, 388) = 1.8$, $p = 0.17$, were significant. The difference between the female and male questionnaire means for each of the PSSUQ scales was only 0.1. Although evidence of gender differences would not affect the usefulness of the PSSUQ, it is of potential interest to practitioners that the instrument did not appear to have an inherent gender bias.

Completeness of Responses to Questionnaire

Neither the main effect, $F(1, 203) = 0.26$, $p = 0.61$, nor the interaction, $F(2, 406) = 1.3$, $p = 0.28$, were significant (see Figure 2.9). The difference between the complete and incomplete questionnaire means for each of the PSSUQ scales was only 0.1. This finding is important because it supports the practice of including partially completed questionnaires when averaging items to compute scale scores (rather than discarding the data from partially completed questionnaires).

Analysis of the distribution of incomplete questionnaires in the analyzed database showed that of 210 total questionnaires, 124 (59%) were
complete and 86 (41%) were incomplete. For the incomplete questionnaires, the mean number of items (with 95% confidence interval bounds)
for Overall (19 items), SysUse (9 items), InfoQual (7 items), and IntQual
(3 items) were, respectively, 15.8 ± 0.5, 8.8 ± 0.1, 4.2 ± 0.5, and 2.9 ± 0.1.
Across the incomplete questionnaires, the completion rate for all SysUse
and IntQual items exceeded 85% (averaging 95% and 97%, respectively);
but the average completion rate for InfoQual items was only 60%. These
data indicate that the primary cause of an incomplete questionnaire was
the failure to complete one or more InfoQual items. In most cases (78%),
these incomplete questionnaires came from dictation studies (which did
not typically include documentation) or standard usability studies conducted on prototypes without documentation.

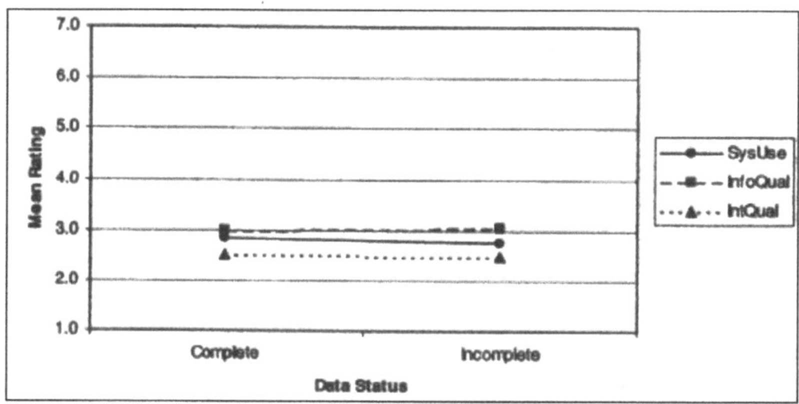

FIGURE 2.9: Completeness by subscale interaction.

Norms

Table 2.4 shows the means and 99% confidence intervals for each item
from this PSSUQ data and from the original PSSUQ and CSUQ data
sets. Figure 2.10 illustrates the patterns of the means for these three sets
of data.

> In later research, documented in Chapter 3 and with practical exam-
> ples in Chapter 5, I took a different approach to establishing norms for
> the PSSUQ/CSUQ, based on correspondence between the CSUQ and
> the SUS, which is the approach I currently recommend for practical
> work with these questionnaires. I've included the findings in Table 2.4
> and Figure 2.10 to provide comprehensive background on the develop-
> ment and assessment of these questionnaires, and to point out some
> interesting normative patterns that appeared across all of the first
> three studies.

There are probably few cases in which practitioners could use these norms for the direct assessment of a product under development. The data for this evaluation came from a variety of sources that included different types of products at different stages of development and the performance of different types of tasks. The original PSSUQ data came from a more consistent source, which included the assessment of three different systems using a set of benchmark tasks developed for the study of office systems performed by participants with different levels of computer experience (for details, see Lewis et al., 1990). The original CSUQ data came from a survey conducted over a broad range of users at IBM. The original PSSUQ and CSUQ data are, however, over 20 years old, which casts some doubt on their usefulness as norms for current systems, even for similar conditions of evaluation.

The consistently better mean ratings in this PSSUQ dataset compared to the original PSSUQ data did not necessarily indicate a wholesale improvement in system usability in the time period between the studies (although this is one possible explanation and might contribute to the dif-ferences). It is also possible that the discrepancies are due to differences in participant populations, system characteristics, or tasks.

Despite this, there were some interesting and potentially useful pat-terns in the means from the three sets of data. The item data showed substantial correlation, with the greatest correlation between the PSSUQ means (CSUQ–PSSUQ current: $r(17) = 0.49$, $p = 0.03$; CSUQ–PSSUQ original: $r(16) = 0.57$, $p = 0.007$; PSSUQ current–PSSUQ original: $r(16) = 0.81$, $p = 0.0005$). For all three sets of data, the item that received the poorest rating—averaging from 0.45 to 0.49 above the next poorest item in the respective set—was Item 9 ("The system gave error messages that

	PSSUQ (Current)			PSSUQ (Original)			CSUQ (Original)		
Item	Lower Limit	Mean	Upper Limit	Lower Limit	Mean	Upper Limit	Lower Limit	Mean	Upper Limit
Q1	2.60	2.85	3.09	3.36	4.00	4.64	3.12	3.30	3.48
Q2	2.45	2.69	2.93	3.40	4.02	4.64	3.36	3.54	3.72
Q3	2.58	2.85	3.11	3.07	3.73	4.40	2.73	2.91	3.09
Q4	2.86	3.16	3.45	3.53	4.15	4.76	3.09	3.27	3.45
Q5	2.79	3.06	3.34	3.37	3.98	4.59	3.05	3.23	3.41
Q6	2.40	2.66	2.91	2.75	3.41	4.07	2.77	2.95	3.13
Q7	2.07	2.27	2.48	2.92	3.57	4.22	3.61	3.82	4.03
Q8	2.54	2.86	3.17	na	na	na	3.40	3.61	3.82
Q9	3.36	3.70	4.05	4.38	4.93	5.48	4.58	4.79	5.00
Q10	2.93	3.21	3.49	3.64	4.18	4.73	3.82	4.03	4.24
Q11	2.65	2.96	3.27	3.87	4.48	5.09	3.94	4.15	4.36
Q12	2.79	3.09	3.38	3.42	4.02	4.63	4.11	4.32	4.53
Q13	2.37	2.61	2.86	3.15	3.79	4.43	3.95	4.13	4.31
Q14	2.46	2.74	3.01	2.81	3.43	4.04	3.70	3.88	4.06
Q15	2.41	2.66	2.92	3.02	3.55	4.08	3.43	3.61	3.79
Q16	2.06	2.28	2.49	2.32	2.91	3.51	3.01	3.19	3.37
Q17	2.18	2.42	2.66	2.37	2.92	3.47	3.02	3.20	3.38
Q18	2.51	2.79	3.07	2.44	3.00	3.56	3.47	3.68	3.89
Q19	2.55	2.82	3.09	3.10	3.69	4.29	3.13	3.31	3.49
SysUse	2.57	2.80	3.02	3.26	3.81	4.36	3.19	3.34	3.49
InfoQual	2.79	3.02	3.24	3.58	4.06	4.54	3.95	4.13	4.31
IntQual	2.28	2.49	2.71	2.42	2.93	3.43	3.17	3.35	3.53
Overall	2.62	2.82	3.02	3.30	3.76	4.22	3.43	3.61	3.79

Note. PSSUQ = Post Study System Usability Questionnaire; CSUQ = Computer System Usability Questionnaire; SysUse = system usefulness; InfoQual = information quality; IntQual = interface quality. Means apear in bold face.

TABLE 2.4: Means and 99% confidence intervals for PSSUQ and CSUQ norms (Versions 1 and 2).

clearly told me how to fix problems"). Finally, mean ratings of InfoQual tend to be higher (poorer) then mean ratings of IntQual, with differences for the three data sets ranging from 0.5 to 1.1. There are several ways in which these findings can be of use to practitioners.

The consistently poor ratings for Item 9 indicate:

- This should not surprise practitioners if they find this in their own data.

- It really is difficult to provide usable error messages throughout a product.

- It may well be worth the effort to make the effort to focus on providing usable error messages.

- If practitioners find the mean for this item to be equal to or less than the mean of the other items in InfoQual, they have been successful in addressing the problem.

The consistent pattern of poor ratings for InfoQual relative to IntQual suggest that practitioners who find this in their data should not necessarily conclude that they have poor documentation or a great interface. On the other hand, if this pattern appeared in the first iteration of a usability evaluation and the developers decided to emphasize improvement to the quality of their information, then any significant decline in the difference between InfoQual and IntQual would be evidence of a successful intervention.

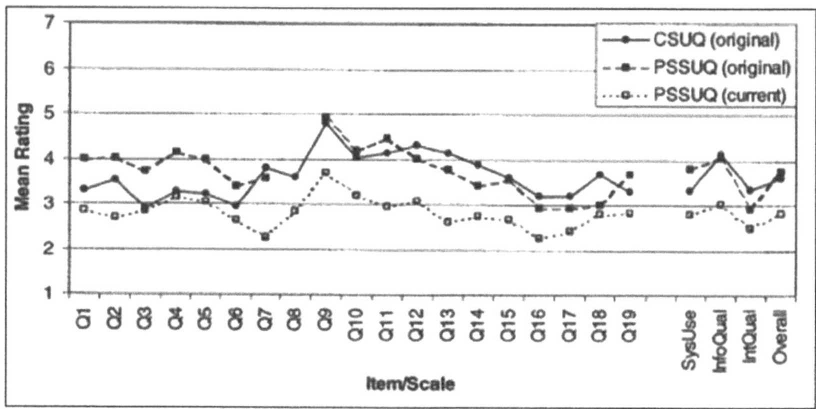

FIGURE 2.10: Completeness by subscale interaction.

Extreme Response Tendency

The extreme response tendency is the tendency to mark the extremes of rating scales rather than points near the middle of the scale. The procedure for determining if a set of responses from a questionnaire exhibits evidence for the extreme response tendency (Nunnally, 1978) is to:

1. Score the responses in two ways – first as the sum of deviations from the center point of the scale using the number of scale steps in the instrument's items, then as the sum of dichotomized scores. Because the PSSUQ uses items with seven scale steps, the effect of dichotomization is that ratings from 1 to 3 become 0, a rating of 4 becomes 0.5; and ratings from 5 to 7 become 1.

2. Divide the squared correlation between the two sets of scores by the product of their internal reliability coefficients (coefficient alphas) to get an estimate of their shared common variances. If that ratio is considerably lower than 1.0 (Nunnally suggested 0.8 as a criterion), it is reasonable to assume that the extremeness tendency is present to some degree.

The obtained ratios for Overall, SysUse, InfoQual, and IntQual were, respectively, .94, 1.02, 1.18, and .95. Because all ratios were greater than .80, there was no evidence for an extremeness tendency for any of the scales. (I also performed the same procedure with truly dichotomous scores, once scoring the central scale point of 4 as 0 and once scoring it as 1. In both cases, the results were essentially the same as with the procedure discussed earlier—no evidence for an extremeness tendency for any of the scales.)

Discussion

The primary purpose of this study was to investigate the similarity between the initially published psychometric properties of the PSSUQ and estimates of the same properties using data from 5 years of lab-based usability evaluation. The key research questions were whether the PSSUQ, used for research in an area very different from that for the previous psychometric evaluations, would exhibit a factor structure, reliability, sensitivity, and norms consistent with the previous research. Successful replication of the previous findings with this new set of data would provide evidence of significant generalizability for the questionnaire, supporting its use by practitioners for measuring participant satisfaction with the usability of tested systems. Failure to replicate would provide information on appropriate limits of generalization for the psychometric properties of the PSSUQ.

Results were Acceptable and Consistent with Previous Research

Although the analyzed data came from studies that differed in both content and protocol from the studies that generated the data for previous analyses, the factor structure, scale reliabilities, and sensitivity analyses were all consistent with prior results and all reached acceptable levels according to standard psychometric criteria. The reliability of IntQual was the most variable across studies, possibly because it has the fewest (only three) items. The profiles of item means across the evaluations also showed strong similarity.

The investigation into the effect of removing Items 3 and 5 from SysUse and Item 13 from InfoQual indicated that the high PSSUQ scale reliabilities were not dependent on the inclusion of these items and that the removal of the items had no substantive effect on the scale means. For these reasons, I began using the shorter versions shown in Chapter 1 in my practice and research. In summary, the analyses supported the continued use by usability practitioners of the PSSUQ and its historical factors as a measure of user perception of and satisfaction with product usability in scenario-based usability evaluations.

PSSUQ Ratings were Insensitive to Gender

Although it would have been acceptable to have detected PSSUQ response differences as a function of gender, the insensitivity of the PSSUQ to gender makes it easier to interpret and report PSSUQ scores because there will typically be no reason to present scores broken down by gender. Despite this, practitioners should still plan to include gender as a variable in their analyses for cases in which different genders might react differently to a product.

PSSUQ Ratings Tended to be Robust Even When Questionnaires were Incomplete

Based on classical psychometric theory, I had hypothesized in earlier articles that the failure to complete all items in the questionnaire should not invalidate the responses or the gathering of the available responses into scale scores by averaging across the available items. The basis for this hypothesis was that, according to psychometric theory, scale reliability is a function of the interrelatedness of scale items, the number of scale steps per item, and the number of items in a scale (Nunnally, 1978). If a participant chooses not to answer an item, the effect should be to reduce slightly the reliability of the scale in that instance; and, in most cases, the remaining items should offer a reasonable estimate of the appropriate scale score. The nonsignificant main effect and interaction for the completeness variable supported this hypothesis and, by extension, my lab's practice of computing mean scale scores from PSSUQs that participants have not fully completed. These data did not provide information concerning how many items a participant could ignore and still produce reliable scale scores. The data did suggest that, in practice, participants typically complete enough items to produce reliable scale scores.

Absolute Normative Data from this Study is of Limited Value, but Normative Patterns can be Useful

Practitioners should be cautious when attempting to interpret their own absolute PSSUQ or CSUQ data against the norms presented in Table 2.4. On the other hand, relative patterns of data that appear consistently in the norms can be of interpretative value. One example is the consistently poor rating for Item 9 ("The system gave error messages that clearly told me how to fix problems"). Another was the consistent difference between the InfoQual and IntQual scores. Because these patterns appeared consistently in the original and these evaluative studies of the PSSUQ and CSUQ, practitioners should expect to find these patterns in their data. Deviations from these patterns are potentially meaningful, especially if the practitioner has focused on the development of clear error messages and high-quality information and finds that the means for these scores are consistent with the means of the other items and scales and are consistent with observed usability problems.

Response Styles and PSSUQ Scores

Of the hypothesized response styles (Nunnally, 1978), the ones that might reasonably affect PSSUQ scores are the acquiescence tendency and the extreme response tendency. The computation of the shared common variance for deviation and dichotomous scores indicated no presence of an extreme response tendency in the current PSSUQ rating data. Nunnally reviewed the evidence for the acquiescence tendency and concluded that it was of little importance as a source of scale invalidity. (Sauro & Lewis, 2011, in research conducted to detect acquiescence if it existed, found no evidence for it.)

Some research (Baumgartner & Steenkamp, 2001; Clarke, 2001; van de Vijver & Leung, 2001) has indicated that there could be significant differences among different cultures with regard to the agreement tendency and the extreme response tendency. Practitioners should avoid using the PSSUQ for the purpose of comparing different cultural groups unless there is evidence that the groups do not differ in these tendencies or the practitioners are prepared to test after the fact for model equivalence (Cheung & Rensvold, 2000). Note that this is not a limitation that applies only to the PSSUQ, but is a limitation of any similar questionnaire if used to compare groups from different cultures.

The strongly nonsignificant outcomes for PSSUQ sensitivity to gender do suggest that, at least in the culture of the United States, there is no difference between men and women with regard to these potential tendencies when completing the PSSUQ. There also appeared to be no such difference between participants who completed all of the PSSUQ items at the end of a study and those who do not. It is interesting that of the seven sensitivity assessments, the PSSUQ exhibited evidence of sensitivity when the method for parsing the data was to divide the systems into different groups (study, developer, stage of development, type of product, type of evaluation). In contrast, the PSSUQ was insensitive when the basis for parsing the data was to divide the respondents into different groups (gender, completeness of responses). This difference was not strongly compelling evidence of a lack of influence of response style on PSSUQ scores (as suggested by Nunnally, 1978, for tests of sentiments in general), but it was consistent with such a hypothesis.

EXPERIMENTAL COMPARISON OF FIVE QUESTIONNAIRES (INCLUDING THE CSUQ)

In 2004, Tullis and Stetson presented the results of an experiment that directly compared the sensitivity of five questionnaires designed to assess perceived usability: standard SUS, QUIS, CSUQ Version 2, Words (a quantification of Microsoft's Product Reaction Cards – see Benedek & Miner, 2002), and Fidelity (a 9-item questionnaire developed and used at Fidelity).

Method

A total of 123 Fidelity employees were randomly assigned to use one of these five questionnaires to rate two financial websites after having completed the same two tasks on each website, with the order of site usage randomized. The tasks were to find the highest price in the past year for a share of a specified company and to find the mutual fund with the highest three-year yield.

Results

Analysis of the overall results for all methods showed a significant preference for Site 1 over Site 2. Tullis and Stetson (2004) then used a Monte Carlo method to randomly select subsamples of the data for each questionnaire at sample sizes of 6, 8, 10, 12, and 14. Their unique sensitivity

test was to see which questionnaire most quickly converged on the conclusion reached with the full sample, where a "correct" conclusion occurred
when a t-test conducted with the sub-sample was statistically significant
and matched the full-sample result.

Figure 2.11 shows that of the five methods assessed in this study, the
SUS was the fastest to converge on the correct conclusion, reaching 75%
agreement at a sample size of 8 and 100% agreement when n = 12. The
CSUQ was the second fastest, reaching 75% agreement at a sample size
of 10 and 90% agreement when n = 12. For the other questionnaires,
even when n = 14 the percentages of correct decisions were in the low- to
mid-70s.

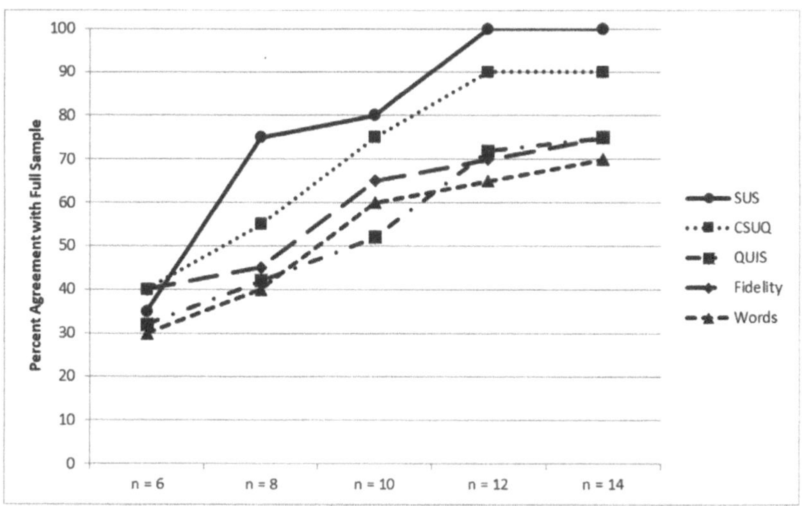

FIGURE 2.11: Sensitivities of five questionnaires that assess perceived usability.

Discussion

These results provided compelling evidence of more efficient discrimina-
tion between designs with the SUS and CSUQ. They also demonstrated
that for this type of study (within-subjects comparison of two designs), it
was possible to obtain statistically significant outcomes with fairly small
sample sizes. Furthermore, this was, as far as I know, the first research
study outside of my lab to investigate a psychometric property of the
CSUQ in any way.

- The initial research into the construct validity of the PSSUQ and CSUQ with three independent sets of data consistently indicated the presence of three underlying factors: SysUse, InfoQual, and IntQual.

- Reliability analyses of the Overall scale and the three factor-based subscales consistently found acceptably high levels of coefficient alpha.

- In the SUMS study, overall PSSUQ scores correlated significantly with ASQ and successful task completion rates averaged across tasks, evidence for concurrent validity.

- Across the early studies, the PSSUQ and CSUQ were sensitive to a large number of variables, including the system used, user group, years of use, range of experience with different systems, stage of system development, and type of evaluation.

- Statistical tests using CSUQ ratings of two financial websites showed rapid convergence of decisions using smaller samples with a full sample (90% agreement when n = 12).

- PSSUQ scores were not sensitive to differences in gender or the completeness of questionnaire responses.

- The PSSUQ and CSUQ, despite being composed just of positive-tone items, did not appear to be affected by response biases (including a quantitative assessment of potential extreme response bias).

- Due to potential cultural differences, avoid using standardized usability questionnaires for the purpose of comparing different cultural groups unless there is evidence that the groups do not differ in response tendencies such as acquiescence or extreme responding.

- Table 2.4 provides preliminary norms for the interpretation of CSUQ scores based on the early research, but should be used with caution by modern practitioners (see Chapters 3 and 4 for a better way to interpret overall PSSUQ and CSUQ scores through reference to SUS norms).

- The patterns of item means in Table 2.4 correlated highly, providing additional evidence for consistency across the studies.

- Two consistent normative patterns across the studies were the relatively poor ratings for "The system gave error messages that clearly told me how to fix problems" and that the mean ratings of InfoQual tend to be poorer than mean ratings of IntQual.

- The consistently poor ratings of the quality of error messages suggest:
    - If this happens in your data, it shouldn't surprise you.
    - It really is difficult to provide usable error messages through-out a product.
    - If you find the mean for this item to be equal to or less than the mean of the other items, you have probably achieved better-than-average error messages.

- The consistent pattern of poor ratings for InfoQual relative to IntQual indicates that if you find this pattern in your data, you shouldn't conclude that you have terrible documentation or a great interface.

- For improved efficiency use the 16-item versions (Version 3) of the PSSUQ and CSUQ (as shown in Chapter 1) instead of the older versions.

## CHAPTER 3

RECENT RESEARCH: 2013-2018

There have been four relatively recent research papers that included the CSUQ: Erdinç and Lewis (2013), Berkman and Karahoca (2016), Lewis (2018b), and Lewis (2018c). The latter three papers had respondents provide concurrent CSUQ and SUS ratings. In addition to informing the research question of whether these two questionnaires assess the construct of perceived usability, they also provided data regarding the correspondence in magnitude of the questionnaires' scores.

The investigation of this correspondence was important because of all the standardized usability questionnaires that are in the public domain, only the SUS has reasonably well-established norms that have been developed and published. Before digging into the details of the more recent CSUQ research, the next section provides information about the SUS and its norms (Sauro & Lewis, 2016; Lewis, 2018d).

THE SUS AND ITS NORMS

The SUS (System Usability Scale) was briefly mentioned in Chapter 1. It was developed in 1984 and initially published in 1996 (Brooke, 2013). Figure 3.1 shows the most commonly used version of the SUS.

The System Usability Scale Standard Version		Strongly Disagree		Strongly Agree
			1 2 3 4 5	
1	I think that I would like to use this system frequently.		O O O O O	
2	I found the system unnecessarily complex.		O O O O O	
3	I thought the system was easy to use.		O O O O O	
4	I think that I would need the support of a technical person to be able to use this system.		O O O O O	
5	I found the various functions in this system were well integrated.		O O O O O	
6	I thought there was too much inconsistency in this system.		O O O O O	
7	I would imagine that most people would learn to use this system very quickly.		O O O O O	
8	I found the system very awkward to use.		O O O O O	
9	I felt very confident using the system.		O O O O O	
10	I needed to learn a lot of things before I could get going with this system.		O O O O O	

FIGURE 3.1: The standard SUS.

Scoring the SUS

The standard approach to scoring the SUS is somewhat complicated due to the alternating tone of the items and to an early decision to manipulate the score to range from 0 to 100. Conceptually, the first scoring step is to convert raw item scores to adjusted scores (also known as "score contributions") that range from 0 (poorest rating) to 4 (best rating), with that adjustment differing for the odd- and even-numbered items (respectively, the positive- and negative-tone items). The scoring system of the SUS requires ratings for all 10 items, so if a respondent leaves an item blank, it should be given a raw score of 3 (the center of the five-point scale). For the odd-numbered items, subtract 1 from the raw score, and for the even-numbered items, subtract the raw score from 5. Compute the sum of the adjusted scores, then multiply by 2.5 to get the standard SUS score. The following equation shows a more concise way to compute a standard SUS score from a set of raw item ratings, using Excel notation:

[3.1] SUS = 2.5(20 + SUM(SUS01,SUS03,SUS05,SUS07,SUS09) − SUM(SUS02,SUS04,SUS06,SUS08,SUS10))

SUS Norms

The paper "An empirical evaluation of the System Usability Scale" (Bangor, Kortum, & Miller, 2008) was a seminal publication in the history of SUS research. Bangor et al. (2008) presented findings based on using the SUS for almost 10 years in the evaluation of numerous products in various phases of development (based on more than 2300 completed SUS questionnaires collected over more than 200 studies). Their analyses and experience indicated that the SUS was a "highly robust and versatile tool for usability professionals" (p. 574).

Given the large amount of SUS data collected over a decade, Bangor et al. (2008) made two attempts at developing norms with their data. About 10% (212) of the completed SUS questionnaires included an 11th item, an adjective rating scale with seven response options: 1: Worst imaginable (n = 1), 2: Awful (n = 0), 3: Poor (n = 15), 4: OK (n = 36), 5: Good (n = 90), 6: Excellent (n = 69), and 7: Best imaginable (n = 1). The SUS means for responses from 3 to 6 (for which n ≥ 15) were, respectively after rounding to the nearest point, 39, 52, 73, and 86. The second approach was an absolute grading scale with A: 90–100, B: 80–89, C: 70–79, D: 60–69, and F: < 60.

Bangor, Kortum, and Miller (2009) increased the sample size of concurrent collection of SUS with the adjective rating scale to almost 1,000 cases. They reported a large and statistically significant correlation of 0.82 between the SUS and the adjective rating scale (evidence of concurrent validity). The means (and parenthetical sample sizes) for the seven response options were:

- 1: Worst imaginable = 12.5 (n = 4)
- 2: Awful = 20.3 (n = 22)
- 3: Poor = 35.7 (n = 72)
- 4: OK = 50.9 (n = 211)
- 5: Good = 71.4 (n = 345)
- 6: Excellent = 85.5 (n = 289)
- 7: Best imaginable = 90.9 (n = 16)

Note that Bangor et al. (2009) expressed some reservation over the interpretation of "OK" (with an associated mean SUS of 50.9) as suggesting an acceptable experience given an overall mean SUS closer to 70 in their large-sample data (Bangor et al., 2008). "In fact, some project team members have taken a score of OK to mean that the usability of the product is satisfactory and no improvements are needed, when scores within the OK range were clearly deficient in terms of perceived usability" (Bangor et al., 2009, p. 120). Their current practice is to anchor this response option with "Fair" instead of "OK" (Phil Kortum, personal communication, 22nd February 2018).

This line of research inspired the development of a curved rather than an absolute grading scale for the SUS (Sauro, 2011; Sauro & Lewis, 2012, 2016). Bangor et al. generously shared their SUS data with Jeff Sauro, as did Tullis and Albert (2008). With this combined data set from 446 studies and over 5000 individual SUS responses, Sauro (2011) used a logarithmic transformation on reflected scores to normalize the distribution, then computed percentile ranks for the entire range of SUS scores. Sauro and Lewis (2016) used those percentile ranks to create the curved grading scale (CGS) shown in Table 3.1.

Note that the average score in the data used to create the Sauro–Lewis CGS was 68, which was by design the exact center of the CGS (a grade of C), but would have been a D in the absolute grading scale. With its 11 grade ranges, the CGS also provides a finer-grained scale than the adjective scale with its seven response options. It addresses the weakness of "OK" in the adjective scale because a 50 would receive an F (clearly deficient) while the lowest value in the range for C (an average experience) is 65. Finally, the CGS is consistent with an industrial practice that has become increasingly common of interpreting a mean SUS of at least 80 (A−) as indicative of an above average user experience. Throughout the rest of this book, letter grades will be from the Sauro–Lewis CGS. Grade values in Table 3.1 are standard numerical assignments for letter grades (https://pages.collegeboard.org/how-to-convert-gpa-4.0-scale).

SUS Score Range	Grade	Grade Value	Percentile Range
84.1 - 100	A+	4.0	96-100
80.8 - 84.0	A	4.0	90-95
78.9 - 80.7	A-	3.7	85-89
77.2 - 78.8	B+	3.3	80-84
74.1 - 77.1	B	3.0	70-79
72.6 - 74.0	B-	2.7	65-69
71.1 - 72.5	C+	2.3	60-64
65.0 -71.0	C	2.0	41-59
62.7 - 64.9	C-	1.7	35-40
51.7 - 62.6	D	1.0	15-34
0.0 - 51.6	F	0.0	0-14

TABLE 3.1: The Sauro-Lewis CGS.

Additional Research on SUS Norms

The Sauro–Lewis CGS provides good general guidance for the interpretation of SUS means. Several lines of research have shown, however, that different types of products and interfaces differ significantly in perceived usability. For example, Sauro (2011) partitioned his data from 446 studies into groups based on product type. See Table 3.2 for the findings (means with confidence intervals, associated CGS grades, and number of studies).

Category	Description	Mean	SD	N	Lower Limit	Upper Limit
Global	Data from the entire set of 446 surveys/studies	68.0	12.5	446	66.5	69.5
B2B	Enterprise software application such as accounting, HR, CRM and order-management systems	67.6	9.2	30	63.0	72.2
B2C	Public facing mass-market consumer software such as office applications, graphics applications, and personal finance software	74.0	7.1	19	69.3	78.7

(continued on pg. 44)

Category	Description	Mean	SD	N	Lower Limit	Upper Limit
Web	Public facing large scale websites (airlines, rental cars, retailers, financial service) and intranets	67.0	13.4	174	64.4	69.6
Cell	Cell phone equipment	64.7	9.8	20	58.4	71.0
HW	Hardware such as phones, modems and Ethernet-cards	71.3	11.1	26	65.2	77.4
Internal SW	Internal productivity software such as customer service and network operations applications	76.7	8.8	21	71.2	82.2
IVR	Interactive Voice Response (IVR) systems, both phone and speech based	79.9	7.6	22	75.3	84.5
Web/IVR	A combination of web-based and interactive voice response systems	59.2	5.5	4	43.1	75.3

TABLE 3.2: SUS benchmarks by type of interface.

Kortum and Bangor (2013) published SUS ratings of overall experience for a set of 14 everyday products from a survey of more than 1000 users. Their findings (means with confidence intervals, associated CGS grades, and number of respondents) appear in Table 3.3.

In 2015, Kortum and Sorber collected SUS ratings from 3,575 users on the usability of 15 mobile applications for phones and tablets (10 based on popularity and 5 that users identified as using frequently). The mean SUS for the top 10 applications was 77.7 (a B+) with a difference of about 20 points between the highest- (87.4, A+) and lowest- (67.7, C) rated applications. This range from grades of C to A+ is skewed to the high end of the scale, but this is likely due to the method used to select the applications for the study (high popularity and high frequency of use).

There are different ways to interpret what these findings (Kortum & Bangor, 2013; Kortum & Sorber, 2015; Sauro, 2011) mean for industrial practice in user experience engineering. They could be interpreted as diminishing the value of the more general norms embodied in the CGS, but a more pragmatic interpretation is that they enhance the general norms. For example, consider the Kortum and Bangor ratings of everyday products. It should not be surprising that a complex spreadsheet program has lower perceived usability than a well-designed search box. For many projects, setting a SUS benchmark of 80 (A−) is reasonable and achievable. If, however, the project is to develop a competitive spreadsheet application, a SUS of 80 is probably unrealistically high (and is probably unrealistically low if developing a new search interface). When possible, practitioners should use a combination of comparison with norms and competitive evaluation when assessing the quality of their products. Practitioners should also exercise some caution when using data from within-subjects studies as benchmarks because respondents who are comparing products may, to a currently unknown extent, give slightly lower ratings to harder products and higher ratings to easier products than they otherwise might.

Product	99% CI Lower Limit	Mean	99% CI Upper Limit	Sauro-Lewis CGS Grade	Std Dev	n
Excel	55.3	56.5	57.7	D	18.6	866
GPS	68.5	70.8	73.1	C to B-	18.3	252
DVR	71.9	74.0	76.1	C+ to B+	17.8	276
PPT	73.5	74.6	75.7	B- to B	16.6	867

(continued on pg. 46)

Product	99% CI Lower Limit	Mean	99% CI Upper Limit	Sauro-Lewis CGS Grade	Std Dev	n
Word	75.3	76.2	77.1	B	15.0	968
Wii	75.2	76.9	78.6	B to B+	17.0	391
iPhone	76.4	78.5	80.6	B to A-	18.3	292
Amazon	80.8	81.8	82.8	A	14.8	801
ATM	81.1	82.3	83.5	A	16.1	731
Gmail	82.2	83.5	84.8	A to A+	15.9	605
Microwaves	86.0	86.9	87.8	A+	13.9	943
Landline phone	86.6	87.7	88.8	A+	12.4	529
Browser	87.3	88.1	88.9	A+	12.2	980
Google search	92.7	93.4	94.1	A+	10.5	948

TABLE 3.3: Kortum and Bangor (2013) SUS ratings of everyday products.

DEVELOPMENT OF A TURKISH VERSION OF THE CSUQ: THE T-CSUQ

While with the Turkish Air Force Academy, Oğuzhan Erdinç decided to translate a standardized usability questionnaire into Turkish to support their UX research, and for that purpose chose the CSUQ. The major qualities that led to the selection of the CSUQ for transformation into a Turkish version included its:

- Desirable psychometric qualities (documented in Chapter 2)

- Successful record of practical and academic applications in its original and modified forms (e.g., Bagheri & Ghorbani, 2009; Chow & Chan, 2010; Frias-Martinez, Chen, & Liu, 2009; Kartakis & Stephanidis, 2010; Periera et al., 2012; Saleem et al., 2011)

- Continuing relevance to current researchers and practitioners – although developed in the late 1980s and first published in the early 1990s, the CSUQ has been cited over 2000 times (Google Scholar, 6/9/2019)

- Applicability in usability evaluation of computer systems in various areas including medicine (Saleem et al., 2011), inclusive e-learning systems (Savidis, Grammenos, & Stephanidis,

2006), clinical learning systems (Chow & Chan, 2010), and 3D land visualization systems (van Lammeren, Houtkamp, Colijn, Hilferink, & Bouwman, 2010), as well as in research into the measurement of the construct of usability (e.g., Christophersen & Konradt, 2011; Finstad, 2010; MacDorman, Whalen, Ho, & Patel, 2011; McNamara & Kirakowski, 2011)

- Intentional multidimensional structure (Bagheri & Ghorbani, 2009; Chow & Chan, 2010; Kartakis & Stephanidis, 2010; Sauro & Lewis, 2016; van Lammeren et al., 2010; in contrast to SUS)

- Noncommercial use (no license fee), which enables researchers and practitioners to perform cost efficient analyses (in contrast to QUIS and SUMI)

Method

Translation of the CSUQ into Turkish

A multidisciplinary research group of reviewers and language professionals adapted the first version of the CSUQ (19 items) into Turkish. The group included two native Turkish reviewers and two bilingual reviewers, a native Turkish language expert, and Oğuzhan Erdinç, who was the group's usability expert and who coordinated the translation process. To initiate the process, he wrote a draft Turkish version of the CSUQ. Next, the research group reviewed the original and the draft Turkish versions through a three-stage review process, modifying the Turkish version to keep the meanings of the items as close as possible to the original.

First stage. The native Turkish and bilingual reviewers independently examined the original and the draft Turkish versions of the CSUQ. They assessed the semantic, idiomatic, and conceptual equivalence of items and identified translation problems such as discrepancies and ambiguities among items. The bilingual reviewers further examined if items in the Turkish version reflected and covered the content of items in the original version.

Among the foremost issues addressed was the similarity between Turkish synonyms of the terms: "effectively," "efficiently," and "productive" used in Items 3, 5 and 8, respectively. The terms used to express effectiveness, efficiency, and productivity in Turkish ("etken," "etkin,"

and "verimli"), used interchangeably in spoken Turkish, were not suffi-
ciently distinctive. The greatest similarity was between Turkish synonyms
of "efficiently" and "productive." The word "verimli" fits "efficiently" in
that in a usability context it means accomplishing tasks with minimum
resources. Another word, "üretken," which is similar to "verimli," was
used in Item 8 for "productive" because it implies producing more outcomes during work. The other issues mostly involved selection of the best
expression and the most suitable form of the verbs. In total, this review
stage led to the modification of 14 items.

Second stage. The version of the T-CSUQ from the first stage was
adapted for usability assessment of web-based course management software used in a state university. Twelve participants (10 students and
two instructors) independently completed the T-CSUQ and provided
comments to indicate any problematic terms and expressions. Also, a
statistician unfamiliar with the software assessed the understandability
of the items. None of the participants reported any major problems with
the clarity of the items.

The Turkish language expert reviewed this tested version of the
T-CSUQ. He assessed the compatibility of the items with the spoken
Turkish language and proposed modifications toward the selection of
the best expression among alternatives. Finally, the two native Turkish
reviewers reassessed the wording of the items independently, with both
of them suggesting minor modifications.

Third stage. The data and reviews from the second stage were used to
revise the T-CSUQ. The primary modification, suggested by the Turkish
language expert, was replacement of the Turkish synonym of "to complete" ("tamamlamak") in Items 3,4,5 and 14 with the Turkish synonym
of "to do" ("yapmak"). Although the former is understandable, the latter
is a better conceptual choice in Turkish. Another significant modification
was to replace "güzel" (initially used for "pleasant" in Item 16) with
"beğenmek" to connote likeability rather than beauty – a more suitable
adjective. Each member of the research group independently reviewed
the original, tested, and revised versions. The research group found the
modifications suitable and reached a consensus about equivalence and
applicability of the items for the final version of the T-CSUQ. Table 3.4
shows the original English and final Turkish versions of the items.

Original Version of CSUQ	Turkish Version of CSUQ
1. Overall, I am satisfied with how easy it is to use this system.	1. Genel olarak, sistemin kullanım kolaylığından memnunum.
2. It is simple to use this system.	2. Sistemi kullanmak basittir.
3. I can effectively complete my work using this system.	3. Sistemi kullanarak işlerimi etkin bir şekilde yapabiliyorum.
4. I am able to complete my work quickly using this system.	4. Sistemi kullanarak işlerimi hızlı bir şekilde yapabiliyorum.
5. I am able to efficiently complete my work using this system.	5. Sistemi kullanarak işlerimi verimli bir şekilde yapabiliyorum.
6. I feel comfortable using this system.	6. Sistemi rahatlıkla kullanabiliyorum.
7. It was easy to learn to use this system.	7. Sistemi kullanmayı öğrenmem kolay oldu.
8. I believe I became productive quickly using this system.	8. Sistemi kullanarak kısa zamanda üretken hale geldiğime inanıyorum.
9. The system gives error messages that clearly tell me how to fix problems.	9. Sistemin verdiği hata mesajları, problemleri nasıl gidereceğimi açıkça anlatmaktadır.
10. Whenever I make a mistake using the system, I recover easily and quickly.	10. Sistemi kullanırken yaptığım hataları, kolay ve hızlı bir şekilde düzeltebiliyorum.
11. The information (such as on-line help, on-screen messages and other documentation) provided with this system is clear.	11. Sistemin verdiği bilgiler (çevrim-içi yardım, ekran mesajları, diğer bilgiler, vb.) açık ve nettir.
12. It is easy to find the information I need.	12. Sistemde ihtiyaç duyduğum bilgilere ulaşmak kolaydır.
13. The information provided with the system is easy to understand.	13. Sistemin verdiği bilgiler kolayca anlaşılmaktadır.
14. The information is effective in helping me complete my work.	14. Sistemin verdiği bilgiler işlerimi yapmama yardımcı olmaktadır.
15. The organization of information on the system screens is clear.	15. Sistemin ekranlarındaki bilgiler açık ve anlaşılır biçimde düzenlenmiştir.
16. The interface of this system is pleasant.	16. Sistemin arayüzünü beğendim.
17. I like using the interface of this system.	17. Sistemin arayüzünü kullanmak hoşuma gidiyor.
18. This system has all the functions and capabilities I expect it to have.	18. Sistem, beklediğim bütün işlevlere sahiptir ve yeterlidir.
19. Overall, I am satisfied with this system.	19. Genel olarak sistem tatmin edicidir.
The anchors:	The anchors:
Strongly agree 1 2 3 4 5 6 7 Strongly disagree	Kesinlikle katılıyorum 1 2 3 4 5 6 7 Kesinlikle katılmıyorum

TABLE 3.4: Items of the CSUQ and their translation into Turkish.

Participants

Even with careful translation of items, there is no guarantee that the T-CSUQ would have the same psychometric properties as the English version (van de Vijver & Leung, 2001). Thus, the next step was to conduct a psychometric evaluation of the T-CSUQ. This evaluation included assessment of reliability, validity, sensitivity, and factor structure for long (Version 1: 19 items) and short (Version 3: 16 items) versions of the questionnaire.

The recommended minimum sample size for psychometric analysis (specifically for factor analysis) is to have at least five participants per item, which, for the 19-item CSUQ, would be 95 participants (Nunnally, 1978). The evaluation process started by inviting the voluntary participation of 120 Turkish employees and managers who used document management software to prepare, sign, and circulate official documents (memos) in a state institution. Participants evaluated this software using the T-CSUQ and had the option to indicate problematic terms and expressions. The return rate was 88.3% (106 questionnaires). Of these, nine questionnaires had missing or invalid data, so the final sample size was 97 (87 male, 10 female), achieving the desired minimum sample size.

The age of the participants ranged between 22 and 42 years with a mean of 30.54 (SD = 4.99). Using 5-point scales, participants also indicated their typical frequency of use of the system (1 = less than one time per day, n = 56; 2 = one to five times per day, n = 8; 3 = six to 10 times per day, n = 8; >10 times per day, n = 5; continuous use, n = 17) and hours of daily use (1 = 0–2, n = 58; 2 = 2–4, n = 13; 4–6, n = 6; 6–8, n = 12; >8 per day, n = 4). Most participants (n = 63) used the system to prepare documents; the remainder (n = 34) used the system to read, initialize, or sign the documents.

Results

Factor Analysis

Table 3.5 shows the varimax-rotated three-factor solution for all 19 items, and Table 3.6 shows the same type of solution for the short version (16 items) that corresponds to the short version of the English CSUQ. Although the item-factor alignment for these two versions of the T-CSUQ was similar to that for the English CSUQ, the structures were not identical. For System Usefulness, seven of eight items aligned as expected (the exception was Item 4). The three Interface Quality items loaded most strongly on the same factor. The alignment discrepancies were especially notable for Information Quality.

To create a short version of the CSUQ-T with item-factor alignment closer to that of the English CSUQ and using the results shown in Table 3.6 as a guide, we conducted a factor analysis on Items 1, 2, 3, 6, 7, and 8 (expected to align with System Usefulness), 9, 11, and 14 (expected to align with Information Quality), and 16, 17, and 18 (expected to align with Interface Quality), plus the overall Item 19. Unfortunately, Item 14 did not align with Information Quality. Substituting Item 13 for 14, as shown in Table 3.7, resulted in a stable Information Quality factor. This is the recommended version of the T-CSUQ.

Item	SysUse	InfoQual	IntQual
1	**0.604**	0.246	0.206
2	**0.735**	0.092	0.257
3	**0.697**	0.272	0.250
4	0.343	0.160	**0.480**
5	**0.588**	0.005	0.475
6	**0.556**	0.241	0.355
7	**0.814**	0.098	0.048
8	**0.680**	0.277	0.089
9	0.384	0.376	0.233
10	**0.510**	0.314	0.336
11	0.291	**0.490**	0.212
12	0.238	0.353	**0.487**
13	0.184	**0.847**	0.242
14	0.191	0.251	**0.527**
15	0.266	0.394	**0.506**
16	0.190	0.271	**0.679**
17	0.187	0.223	**0.625**
18	0.082	0.092	**0.640**
19	0.163	0.045	**0.747**

TABLE 3.5: Varimax-rotated three-factor solution for 19-item T-CSUQ.

Item	SysUse	InfoQual	IntQual
1	**0.589**	0.192	0.241
2	**0.609**	0.338	0.193
4	0.429	0.041	**0.558**
6	**0.629**	0.025	0.430
7	**0.849**	0.160	0.029
8	**0.694**	0.260	0.103
9	0.294	**0.632**	0.156
10	**0.549**	0.208	0.385
11	0.284	**0.470**	0.216
12	0.297	0.174	**0.547**

(continued on pg. 52)

Item	SysUse	InfoQual	IntQual
14	0.061	**0.518**	0.466
15	0.276	0.398	**0.508**
16	0.169	0.259	**0.677**
17	0.170	0.203	**0.633**
18	0.068	0.138	**0.634**
19	0.141	0.178	**0.690**

TABLE 3.6: Varimax-rotated three-factor solution for 16-item T-CSUQ.

Original #	New #	SysUse	InfoQual	IntQual
1	1	**0.608**	0.270	0.228
2	2	**0.672**	0.197	0.234
3	3	**0.651**	0.364	0.230
6	4	**0.551**	0.235	0.360
7	5	**0.857**	0.072	0.051
8	6	**0.686**	0.286	0.063
9	7	0.334	**0.499**	0.162
11	8	0.249	**0.551**	0.166
13	9	0.195	**0.720**	0.252
15	10	0.164	0.327	**0.697**
16	11	0.174	0.260	**0.628**
17	12	0.083	0.095	**0.630**
18	13	0.178	0.068	**0.684**

TABLE 3.7: Varimax-rotated three-factor solution for final (13-item) version of the T-CSUQ.

Reliability

Coefficient alphas for the recommended short version (SV) of the T-CSUQ (using the new numbering in Table 3.7) exceeded the minimum criterion of 0.70, indicating sufficient reliability for its intended use:

- Overall (Items 1–13): 0.85
- System Usefulness (Items 1–6): 0.88
- Information Quality (Items 7–9): 0.71
- Interface Quality (Items 10–12): 0.73

Sensitivity

Consistent with the results of sensitivity analyses of the English CSUQ (Lewis, 2002), t-tests indicated no evidence of an effect of gender on ratings for any of the scales (all $p > 0.9$). There were marginal effects of the type of work (preparing vs. reading/signing documents) on System Usefulness, $t(95) = 1.6$, $p = 0.10$, and Overall, $t(95) = 1.75$, $p = 0.08$, but not for Information Quality, $t(95) = 0.58$, $p = 0.56$, or Interface Quality, $t(95) = 0.95$, $p = 0.35$.

Analyses of frequency of use and duration of daily use provided strong evidence of scale sensitivity. Because the sample sizes for some frequency and duration groups were relatively small, we dichotomized these variables to get the number of participants in each group as equal as possible (Frequency of Use: $n = 56$ "not every day" vs. $n = 38$ "every day"; Duration of Use: $n = 58$ "<2 hours per day" vs. $n = 35$ ">2 hours per day").

As shown in Figure 3.2, a mixed-model analysis of variance (using T-CSUQ-SV scales as a within-subjects variable) indicated a significant main effect of frequency of use, $F(1, 92) = 10.3$, $p = 0.002$; a significant main effect of scale, $F(2, 2) = 3.7$, $p = 0.026$; and a significant interaction, $F(2, 2) = 3.7$, $p = 0.026$.

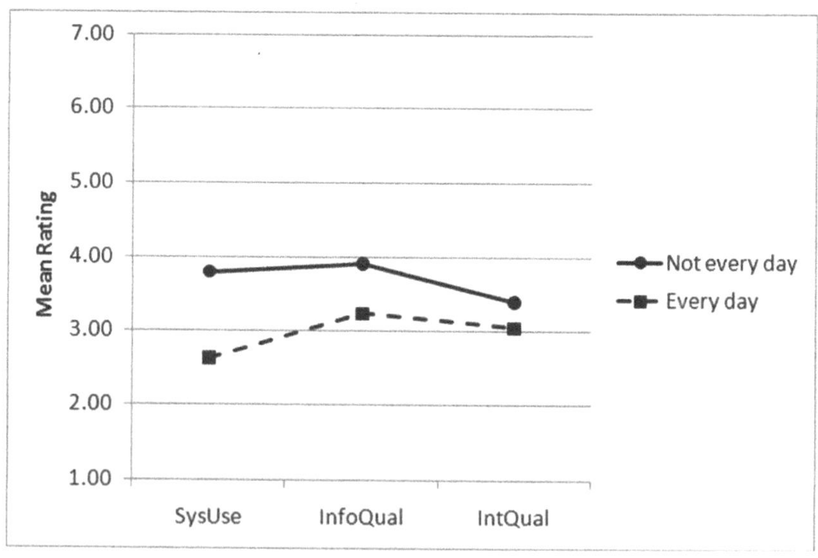

FIGURE 3.2: Scale by frequency of use for the T-CSUQ-SV.

Figure 3.3 shows the results of a similar analysis of duration of use, which had significant main effects of duration, $F(1, 91) = 30.8$, $p = 0.0000003$, and scale, $F(2, 2) = 3.8$, $p = 0.025$, but no significant interaction, $F(2, 2) = 2.1$, $p = 0.12$. Participants who used the system more frequently or for longer daily durations tended to rate the system more favorably.

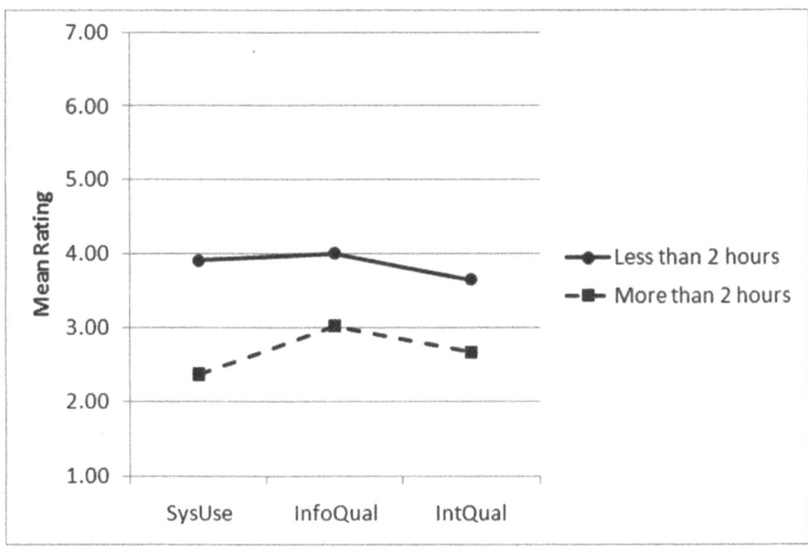

FIGURE 3.3: Scale by daily duration of use for the T-CSUQ-SV.

Extreme Response Tendency

Of particular interest was whether the Turkish sample would show evidence of a tendency toward an extreme response bias. Investigation of this for the English version of the CSUQ indicated no extreme response tendency (Lewis, 2002), but there is some evidence that members of different cultures exhibit different levels of the extreme response tendency, although these differences do not always appear (Grimm & Church, 1999). Nunnally's (1978) method (described in Chapter 2) for assessing the extreme response tendency indicated no evidence for such a response bias. All ratios of squared correlations to products of coefficient alpha for deviation and dichotomous scores were greater than 1 (ratios less than 0.8 indicate an extreme response tendency).

Final Version of the Questionnaire

Based on the psychometric evaluation, the T-CSUQ-SV contains 13 items, as shown in Figure 3.4. Note the renumbering of the items from 1 to 13. For the original item numbers, refer to Table 3.4.

	The T-CSUQ Short Version 1	Kesinlikle katılıyorum								Kesinlikle katılmıyorum
		1	2	3	4	5	6	7		NA
1	Genel olarak, sistemin kullanım kolaylığından memnunum.	O	O	O	O	O	O	O		O
2	Sistemi kullanmak basittir.	O	O	O	O	O	O	O		O
3	Sistemi kullanarak işlerimi etkin bir şekilde yapabiliyorum.	O	O	O	O	O	O	O		O
4	Sistemi rahatlıkla kullanabiliyorum.	O	O	O	O	O	O	O		O
5	Sistemi kullanmayı öğrenmem kolay oldu.	O	O	O	O	O	O	O		O
6	Sistemi kullanarak kısa zamanda üretken hale geldiğime inanıyorum.	O	O	O	O	O	O	O		O
7	Sistemin verdiği hata mesajları, problemleri nasıl gidereceğimi açıkça anlatmaktadır.	O	O	O	O	O	O	O		O
8	Sistemin verdiği bilgiler (çevrim-içi yardım, ekran mesajları, diğer bilgiler, vb.) açık ve nettir.	O	O	O	O	O	O	O		O
9	Sistemin verdiği bilgiler kolayca anlaşılmaktadır.	O	O	O	O	O	O	O		O
10	Sistemin arayüzünü beğendim.	O	O	O	O	O	O	O		O
11	Sistemin arayüzünü kullanmak hoşuma gidiyor.	O	O	O	O	O	O	O		O
12	Sistem, beklediğim bütün işlevlere sahiptir ve yeterlidir.	O	O	O	O	O	O	O		O
13	Genel olarak sistem tatmin edicidir.	O	O	O	O	O	O	O		O

FIGURE 3.4: Final version of the T-CSUQ.

Discussion

The primary goal of this research was to develop a standardized usability questionnaire for use by speakers of the Turkish language. Through a careful multistage translation process and psychometric evaluation, this research produced a questionnaire, the T-CSUQ-SV, based on the well-known CSUQ. It is important to note that the T-CSUQ-SV is not a simple item-for-item translation of the CSUQ. Only 13 of the original 19 items survived the process of the transformation of the CSUQ into the T-CSUQ-SV.

Psychometric evaluation of the T-CSUQ-SV indicated an acceptable level of reliability for the overall scale and its subscales (all coefficient ⍺s > .70). Factor analysis indicated appropriate construct validity, with the items for each subscale loading on separate factors. Consistent with psychometric evaluations of the English CSUQ, the T-CSUQ-SV was insensitive to gender, moderately sensitive to type of usage, and highly sensitive to frequency and duration of use. Also consistent with the English version of the CSUQ, there was no evidence that respondents exhibited an extreme response tendency, allaying potential concerns with cross-cultural use of questionnaires raised by Baumgartner and Steenkamp (2001), Cheung and Rensvold (2000), Clarke (2001), and van de Vijver and Leung (2001). These results indicate that Turkish usability practitioners should be able to use the T-CSUQ-SV with confidence when conducting user research.

THE INITIAL ASSESSMENT OF THE CORRESPONDENCE BETWEEN THE CSUQ AND THE SUS

In 2016 Berkman and Karahoca investigated the relationship between the Usability Metric for User Experience (UMUX; Finstad, 2010; UMUX-LITE: Lewis, Utesch, & Maher, 2013) and other measures of perceived usability, including the SUS and the CSUQ.

Method

The standard SUS and the CSUQ (Version 3) were included in a survey developed at Bahcessehir University in Turkey. The 151 respondents (65 native speakers of English and 86 non-native) rated one of three mind map applications. Because the respondents had sufficient fluency in English, Berkman and Karahoca used the English CSUQ (Version 3) rather than the T-CSUQ (Erdinç and Lewis, 2013). The majority of the respondents (74%) reported having developed mind maps with the software at least 20 times.

Results

The reliability (coefficient alpha) of the overall CSUQ was 0.95. Factor analysis found the expected alignment between items and factors, evidence of construct validity. The CSUQ (overall and subscales) correlated significantly with UMUX-related and SUS scores (strongest correlation was with SysUse), providing evidence of concurrent validity. Sensitivity analyses of the CSUQ found effects of age group, product, and levels of experience. The CSUQ means did not differ by gender.

To assess the correspondence between the means, it's helpful to use Equation 3.2 to convert the CSUQ to a metric that, like the SUS, can range from 0 to 100 where higher scores indicate a better user experience. Breaking down the equation, the process of getting from a traditional CSUQ score to one that matches the SUS involves subtracting 1 from the mean of the 16 individual CSUQ items and multiplying that by 100/6 to stretch it out to a 0–100-point scale, then subtracting from 100 to reverse the scale. For example, if the mean CSUQ was 1 (the best possible standard CSUQ mean), the transformed score would be 100 (100 - (1 - 1) (100/6) = 100 - 0 = 100). If the mean CSUQ was 7 (the worst possible standard CSUQ mean), the transformed score would be 0 (100 - (7 - 1) (100/6) = 100 - 100 = 0). For a mean CSUQ of 4 (the center of the standard CSUQ 7-point scale), the transformed score would be 50 (100 - (4 - 1) (100/6) = 100 - 50 = 50).

[3.2] CSUQ100 = 100 - ((((CSUQ01+CSUQ02+CSUQ03+CSUQ04+
CSUQ05+CSUQ06+CSUQ07+CSUQ08+CSUQ09+CSUQ10+
CSUQ11+CSUQ12+CSUQ13+CSUQ14+CSUQ15+CSUQ16)/16)-
1)/100/6

Overall, the mean SUS was 79.5 and the mean CSUQ was 2.2. Applying Equation 3.2, the standard CSUQ mean of 2.2 transformed to a CSUQ100 of 80.0, which was almost equal to the mean SUS of 79.5. Using the Sauro-Lewis CGS (Table 3.1), both means received a grade of A-. Table 3.8 shows means as a function of a variety of independent variables, with a focus on mean differences (SUS - CSUQ100) for 0-100-point scores and grade point averages (GPA) for the associated CGS grades.

Discussion

This study, conducted in Turkey and assessing a new type of software, provided evidence of acceptable psychometric quality for Version 3 of the CSUQ, including replication of its construct validity and overall reliability. The overall CSUQ and SUS means had very close correspondence. Examination of Table 3.8 shows that this close correspondence was typical for the various ways of partitioning the data into independent groups (where "independent" means no individual was a member of more than one group). For the groups with larger sample sizes (n > 20), in no case was the absolute difference between CSUQ and SUS means greater than 3, and in no case was the absolute difference in the mean CGS GPA greater than 0.7 – less than a grade level.

The results greatly extended the generalizability of use of the CSUQ from a psychometric perspective (reliability and validity). Even more important, the data indicated enough correspondence between concurrently collected SUS and CSUQ scores to justify using the CGS norms that were initially developed for the interpretation of SUS means to interpret the CSUQ means, especially when the sample sizes were reasonably large (n > 20). This was, however, just one study, making it a bit early to claim that the correspondence findings would generalize to other research settings.

REPLICATING THE ORIGINAL CSUQ SURVEY AND CSUQ/SUS CORRESPONDENCE

Early in 2018 I conducted research to (1) replicate the original CSUQ survey (Lewis, 1995, summarized in Chapter 2) with the CSUQ Version 3 and (2) extend Berkman and Karahoca's (2016) investigation of correspondence between the CSUQ and the SUS (summarized above). This is an issue of both theoretical and practical significance. From a theoretical perspective, if the CSUQ and SUS – possibly the two most popular instruments for the assessment of perceived usability – did not appear to substantially measure the same thing, then what would that mean for the validity of the construct of usability (Lewis, 2018a; Tractinsky, 2017)? From a practical perspective, if they do essentially measure the same thing, then practitioners should be able to put data from both questionnaires on a common scale for interpretation as indicating relatively poor, average, or good levels of perceived usability based on the grading scale norms developed for the SUS (Table 3.1).

Method

The Survey

Respondents completed a Survey Gizmo (surveygizmo.com) designed to recreate the CSUQ survey mailed out to IBM employees for the research reported in Lewis (1995), but with the addition of the SUS and the UMUX. The instructions to participants were

Thank you for agreeing to participate in this evaluation. It should take about 5-10 minutes to complete this survey. In this survey, you'll use a variety of standardized usability questionnaires to rate the primary computer system (hardware, software, and documentation) that you use for your work. Full disclosure – I am in no position to help with problems you might be having with your system – you'll need to work with your management and IBM service to resolve anything like that. My primary goal is to understand the statistical relationships among these different questionnaires.

Comparison	Values	n	CSUQ	CSUQ100
Overall	NA	151	2.2	80.0
Gender	Male	113	2.2	80.0
	Female	38	2.2	80.0
	Mean			
Age	<25	15	2.5	75.0
	25-29	7	2.2	80.0
	30-34	6	2.0	83.3
	35-39	21	2.0	83.3
	40-44	23	2.3	78.3
	45-49	24	2.4	76.7
	50-54	19	2.1	81.7
	55-59	16	2.1	81.7
	60-64	14	2.5	75.0
	65-69	6	1.9	85.0
	Mean			
	<40	49	2.2	80.4
	40+	102	2.2	79.7
	Mean			
English	Non-	86	2.3	78.3
	Native	65	2.1	81.7
	Mean			
Usage	Once	3	2.2	80.0
	2-4	13	2.5	75.0
	5-10	12	2.8	70.0
	11-15	8	3.4	60.0
	16-20	4	2.2	80.0
	>20	111	2.1	81.7
	Mean			
	1-10	28	2.5	75.0
	11+	123	2.6	73.9
	Mean			
System	MM01	45	2.0	83.3
	MM02	73	2.3	78.3
	MM03	33	2.4	76.7
	Mean			

TABLE 3.8: CSUQ correspondence with SUS overall and for a variety of independent variables.

SUS	Diff (S-C)	CGS: CSUQ	CGS: SUS	GPA: CSUQ	GPA: SUS	Diff (S-C)
79.5	-0.5	A-	A-	3.7	3.7	0.0
78.6	-1.4	A-	B+	3.7	3.3	-0.4
82.1	2.1	A-	A	3.7	4.0	0.3
	0.3					*-0.1*
77.0	2.0	B	B	3.0	3.0	0.0
75.4	-4.6	A-	B	3.7	3.0	-0.7
85.8	2.5	A	A+	4.0	4.0	0.0
80.4	-2.9	A	A-	4.0	3.7	-0.3
78.8	0.5	B+	B+	3.3	3.3	0.0
78.4	1.7	B	B+	3.0	3.3	0.3
80.0	-1.7	A	A-	4.0	3.7	-0.3
77.5	-4.2	A	B+	4.0	3.3	-0.7
81.4	6.4	B	A	3.0	4.0	1.0
86.3	1.3	A+	A+	4.0	4.0	0.0
	0.1					*-0.1*
79.7	-0.8	A-	A-	3.7	3.7	0.0
80.4	0.7	A-	A-	3.7	3.7	0.0
	0.0					*0.0*
78.0	-0.3	B+	B+	3.3	3.3	0.0
81.4	-0.3	A	A	4.0	4.0	0.0
	-0.3					*0.0*
80.0	0.0	A-	A-	3.7	3.7	0.0
78.7	3.7	B	B+	3.0	3.3	0.3
73.8	3.8	C	B-	2.0	2.7	0.7
66.9	6.9	D	C	1.0	2.0	1.0
72.5	-7.5	A-	C+	3.7	2.3	-1.4
81.3	-0.4	A	A	4.0	4.0	0.0
	1.1					*0.1*
77.5	2.5	B	B+	3.0	3.3	0.3
73.6	-0.3	C+	C+	2.3	2.3	0.0
	1.1					*0.2*
82.8	-0.5	A	A	4.0	4.0	0.0
77.5	-0.8	B+	B+	3.3	3.3	0.0
79.3	2.6	B	A-	3.0	3.7	0.7
	0.4					*0.2*

Please keep in mind that you are participating in an evaluation of the usability of computer systems. This is not a test of you – you are helping us to understand the relationships among various ways of measuring perceived usability. Please try to answer all the items in the questionnaires, but don't spend a lot of time on an item – your first impression is fine. The items will differ in whether a low number or a high number indicates a good or poor user experience, so please read each item carefully.

OK, let's get started.

Respondents then completed, in this order, the CSUQ (see Figure 1.2), the SUS (see Figure 3.1), and the UMUX (Finstad, 2010), then completed a demographics section that included system questions [type of hardware, operating system (OS), and applications used] and respondent characteristics (length of time at IBM, length of time using the rated system, and frequency of system use).

The Respondents

Respondents were members of the IBM User Experience panel. To form the panel, invitations were emailed to 20,000 randomly selected IBM employees (US only). About 10% (2035) of those invited agreed to join the panel. Of these 2035 members, 746 (36.7%) completed the survey. In accordance with the rules established by their developers, missing data in the CSUQ were left unchanged while missing data in the SUS and UMUX were replaced with the center item of the rating scale (three for the SUS, four for the UMUX).

Referring back to the survey instruction, "The items will differ in whether a low number or a high number indicates a good or poor user experience, so please read each item carefully" – despite providing numerous instructions throughout the survey regarding item format, a comparison of the ratings of a CSUQ item (#2) and a similar SUS item (#3) (both ratings of system ease of use) indicated that 128 (about 17%) of the respondents who completed the survey provided radically different ratings for their systems' ease of use with those two items (more than a 50-point difference after conversion of both items to a common 0–100-point scale). This is a strong indication that they did not notice the shift in item formats from the CSUQ to the SUS, so their data were deleted before conducting any further analyses, leaving a data set with 618 cases. All statistical analyses used SPSS Version 24 (IBM Corporation, Armonk, NY).

Results

Note that for this book, the focus is on the relationship between the CSUQ and the SUS. The UMUX-related results are not relevant, so they are not included.

Reliability

All of the questionnaires had values of coefficient alpha consistent with the prior literature. The values of coefficient alpha computed for the questionnaires were 0.97 for the CSUQ (with 0.95, 0.93, and 0.91, respectively, for the SysUse, InfoQual, and IntQual subscales), and 0.93 for the SUS.

Concurrent Validity

The correlation between concurrently collected CSUQ and SUS scores was 0.76, with 0.74, 0.65, and 0.68 respectively for the SysUse, InfoQual, and IntQual subscales (all correlations statistically significant with $p < 0.0001$ and 616 degrees of freedom).

Construct Validity

As shown in Table 3.9, analyses of the CSUQ ratings (using unrestricted least-squares factor analysis) were consistent with previous research (Berkman & Karahoca, 2016; Lewis, 1995, 2002). Parallel analysis (O'Connor, 2000) indicated a three-factor solution would be appropriate, and items strongly aligned on factors as expected (1–6, 7–12, and 13–15). As expected when using summative metrics (Cliff, 1987; Nunnally, 1978), there were significant ($p < 0.0001$, $df = 616$) correlations among the subscales (SysUse-InfoQual: 0.71; SysUse-IntQual: 0.80; InfoQual-IntQual: 0.71).

Correspondence between the CSUQ and SUS

To examine the correspondence between the magnitude of CSUQ and SUS scores, CSUQ scores were converted from their historical scale of a value between 1 and 7 (where a lower number indicates a better experience) to a 0–100-point scale to match the SUS, using Formula [3.2]. With this transformation, the overall mean CSUQ was 66.7 and the mean SUS was 68.7 – a difference of 2 points on a 101-point scale. Given the fairly large sample size, this was a statistically significant difference ($t(617) = 3.2$, $p = 0.001$), but matching these scores against the Sauro–Lewis CGS (Table 3.1) shows that they would both receive a grade of C, so from a user experience perspective there was not a practically significant difference.

Item	SysUse	InfoQual	IntQual
1	**0.81**	0.29	0.35
2	**0.81**	0.34	0.29
3	**0.71**	0.32	0.35
4	**0.76**	0.22	0.32
5	**0.75**	0.36	0.23
6	**0.78**	0.41	0.23
7	0.22	**0.77**	0.14
8	0.45	**0.64**	0.25
9	0.22	**0.84**	0.25
10	0.32	**0.76**	0.23
11	0.32	**0.77**	0.24
12	0.43	**0.62**	0.37
13	0.46	0.33	**0.71**
14	0.49	0.34	**0.76**
15	**0.48**	0.41	**0.51**
16	**0.65**	0.43	**0.53**

TABLE 3.9: Varimax-rotated factor analysis of CSUQ Version 3.

It is also interesting that the mean SUS of this data set was 68.7 – very close to the center of the CGS (68), which indicates that the average user in this sample reported an average level of perceived usability. The values of similarly transformed CSUQ subscale means (SysUse: 73.8, InfoQual: 56.4, IntQual: 71.3) suggested that none of them had close enough correspondence with the SUS to warrant interpreting them with the CGS.

One of the system variables for which there was a statistically significant difference was the OS. The mean for respondents using an Apple© system was higher than that for those using a Windows© system for both the CSUQ and the SUS (CSUQ: t(560) = 6.4, p < 0.0001; SUS: t(560) = 5.2, p < 0.0001). The means and corresponding CGS grades were:

- Apple, CSUQ: 76.6 (B)
- Apple, SUS: 76.8 (B)
- Windows, CSUQ: 64.1 (C–)
- Windows, SUS: 66.9 (C)

The CSUQ and SUS CGS grades were the same for the Apple respondents (both B) and were within a fractional grade boundary for Windows respondents (C– and C).

Discussion

The CSUQ and the SUS are two of the most-used standardized questionnaires for the assessment of perceived usability. Both were developed with a common goal, but in different places by different groups of researchers. On their faces, they are quite different. The CSUQ (Version 3) has 16 items; the SUS has 10. The CSUQ has well-defined subscales in addition to its overall measurement; the SUS does not. The CSUQ items all have a positive tone with 7-point end-anchored scales that include NA outside the scale; the standard SUS is a mixed-tone questionnaires with 5-point end-anchored scales and no NA response option. The rules for computing CSUQ scores do not require any special treatment of missing values, but for the SUS the recommended procedure is to replace missing values with the center point of its scales (3).

Despite these structural differences, the CSUQ and SUS correlated highly. In other words, they appear to be measuring essentially the same thing. Given the goals of their developers and the content of their items, that "thing" is presumably the construct of perceived usability. In addition to this, the correspondence in the magnitude of their measurements when placed on a consistent 0–100-point scale was striking. Despite a statistically significant but small deviation between SUS and CSUQ scores, conversion to letter grades using the CGS showed a remarkable consistency in assigned grades.

One of the most important aspects of using the SUS for practical usability assessment is the development of open source norms, starting with data published by Bangor et al. (2008) and Tullis and Albert (2008), to which Sauro and Lewis (2016) added additional data to derive their CGS. The finding that transformed CSUQ scores appeared to closely correspond to concurrently collected SUS scores means that usability practitioners who use CSUQ (and by extension, the PSSUQ) can, with reasonable confidence, use the Sauro–Lewis CGS as an indication of relatively poor, average, or good levels of perceived usability.

As discussed above and summarized in Table 3.3, Kortum and Bangor (2013) published research on retrospective ratings of 14 everyday products and product classes using the SUS. They used an online survey to collect data during 2010–2011 from just over 1,000 respondents, with those respondents about evenly split between Rice University undergraduate students and participants recruited using Amazon's Mechanical Turk. There were statistically significant differences in mean SUS ratings between the Rice and Turk groups for eight products, but the means across all 14 products were almost identical (79.2 for Rice; 79.6 for Turk) and the correlation of the scores across products for the two groups was very high ($r(12) = 0.95$, $p < 0.0001$). One of the strongest factors affecting the ratings was the amount of experience respondents reported having with the product, but the higher the average SUS score, the less experience mattered, indicating that "products that have superior usability are usable by novices and experts alike, whereas hard to use products may get easier over time but never reach superior usability even with heavy experience" (p. 74).

As part of a continuing investigation into the relationships among various measures of perceived usability, a major goal of this study was to replicate the method of Kortum and Bangor (2013) for a subset of their everyday products that were (1) likely to have been used by members of the IBM User Experience panel and (2) had a wide range of mean SUS ratings reported by Kortum and Bangor – specifically, Excel (56.5), Word (76.2), Amazon (81.8), and Gmail (83.5). In addition to exploring the similarities and differences in independent SUS ratings of these products seven years later with a different population of users, this provides an opportunity to measure the correspondence between SUS and CSUQ scores.

To summarize, the primary research goals were to investigate:

- The relationship between the SUS scores reported by Kortum and Bangor (2013) for four everyday products (Excel, Word, Amazon, and Gmail) and those collected in this study.

- The correlation and correspondence of the CSUQ with the SUS for these everyday products.

The Survey

The survey design and instructions were the same as those for the previous study replicating the original CSUQ survey (summarized in the previous section of this chapter). For each of the four products, there were three versions of the survey which differed in the order of presentation of the usability questionnaires (Latin square design: CSUQ/SUS/UMUX, SUS/UMUX/CSUQ, UMUX/CSUQ/SUS). After random assignment to a survey version and for each product with which they had experience, respondents completed the three usability questionnaires and a section which included system questions (type of hardware, operating system, and applications used) and usage characteristics (length of time using the rated product and frequency of product use). In accordance with the rules established by their developers, missing data in the CSUQ were left unchanged while missing data in the SUS were replaced with the center item of the rating scale (3). Responses to the CSUQ were used to compute scores for each of its subscales and the overall CSUQ, transformed to 0-100-point scales using Equation [3.2]. All statistical analyses used SPSS Version 25.

The Respondents

Respondents were members of the IBM User Experience panel (described in the previous section of this chapter). Due to membership attrition, at the time of this study, there were 1897 members of the panel. As a check on data quality, cases in which respondents had more than a 50-point difference among the SUS and CSUQ scores (after translation to a common 0–100 point scale) were removed due to the likelihood that those respondents had made rating errors due to the different questionnaire formats. The resulting sample sizes for each product (and the percentage of the total panel) were:

- Excel: 390 (20.6%)
- Word: 453 (23.9%)
- Amazon: 338 (17.8%)
- Gmail: 256 (13.5%)

Results

Reliability

Across all data, the values of coefficient alpha computed for the questionnaires were 0.97 for the CSUQ (with 0.96, 0.93, and 0.90, respectively, for the SysUse, InfoQual, and IntQual subscales), and 0.94 for the SUS. The overall data are dependent to some unknown degree due to the preservation of respondent anonymity and the possibility that some respondents rated more than product. Within products, though, the data were independent. Table 3.10 shows the estimated reliabilities for each product.

Product	CSUQ	SysUse	InfoQual	IntQual	SUS
Excel	0.96	0.95	0.91	0.88	0.93
Word	0.97	0.96	0.93	0.90	0.94
Amazon	0.97	0.96	0.93	0.91	0.94
Gmail	0.97	0.96	0.05	0.89	0.93

TABLE 3.10: Coefficient alpha for CSUQ and SUS for each product.

Concurrent Validity

Across all data, as shown in Table 3.11, the correlation between concurrently collected CSUQ and SUS scores was 0.87, with 0.87, 0.73, and 0.78 respectively for the SysUse, InfoQual, and IntQual subscales (all correlations statistically significant with p < 0.0001 and at least 1434 degrees of freedom).

Product	CSUQ	SysUse	InfoQual	IntQual
Excel	0.87	0.87	0.70	0.75
Word	0.85	0.86	0.66	0.81
Amazon	0.86	0.86	0.75	0.81
Gmail	0.88	0.85	0.77	0.76

TABLE 3.11: CSUQ correlation with SUS for each product (all p < 0.0001 with > 250 df).

Construct Validity

Across all data, factor analysis of the CSUQ ratings (using unrestricted least squares factor analysis) was consistent with previous research (Berkman & Karahoca, 2016; Lewis, 1995, 2002, 2018b), with Items 1–6 aligning on the first factor, 7–12 aligning on the second, 13–15 aligning on the third, and 16 aligning on multiple factors (see Table 3.12). Table 3.13 shows the factor structures for the data from each product. The factor analyses at the product level showed some minor inconsistencies with the expected factor structure, but those inconsistencies were not themselves consistent across the four analyses.

Item	SysUse	InfoQual	IntQual
1	**0.78**	0.29	0.38
2	**0.77**	0.35	0.22
3	**0.79**	0.28	0.35
4	**0.79**	0.23	0.37
5	**0.74**	0.42	0.21
6	**0.76**	0.35	0.30
7	0.22	**0.73**	0.14
8	0.47	**0.63**	0.26
9	0.22	**0.85**	0.20
10	0.30	**0.77**	0.31
11	0.34	**0.73**	0.30
12	0.37	**0.57**	**0.53**
13	0.40	0.37	**0.74**
14	0.44	0.37	**0.75**
15	**0.50**	0.21	**0.52**
16	**0.65**	0.30	**0.57**

TABLE 3.12: CSUQ factor analysis across products.

Sensitivity

Sensitivity was assessed by conducting a series of ANOVAs for a variety of independent variables and holding constant in each analysis the independent variables of Subscale (SysUse, InfoQual, and IntQual) and Product (Excel, Word, Amazon, and Gmail). You would expect each analysis to have significant main effects of Subscale and Product and their interaction. Evidence of sensitivity would be indicated by significant main effects of the other independent variables or their interactions with Subscale and/or Product.

Operating system. There was a marginally significant main effect of operating system ($F(1, 1354) = 2.9$, $p = 0.09$). The Apple mean was 73.1 (B-) and the Windows mean was 75.2 (B).

Time used. The main effect of the amount of time respondents reported using the products was statistically significant ($F(2, 1414) = 4.2$, $p = 0.016$), as was its interaction with Subscale ($F(4, 2828) = 2.8$, $p = 0.25$; see Figure 3.5). Its interaction with Product was marginally significant ($F(6, 1414) = 2.0$, $p = 0.065$. The mean for 0-5 years of use was 72.3 (C+), for 6-10 years was 72.4 (C+), and for more than 10 years was 75.9 (B).

	Excel			Word		
Item	SysUse	InfoQual	IntQual	SysUse	InfoQual	IntQual
1	**0.75**	0.23	0.46	**0.85**	0.30	0.25
2	**0.73**	0.35	0.23	**0.76**	0.27	0.22
3	**0.76**	0.20	0.47	**0.88**	0.24	0.24
4	**0.72**	0.15	0.52	**0.88**	0.22	0.22
5	**0.66**	0.43	0.21	**0.77**	0.41	0.19
6	**0.77**	0.31	0.32	**0.79**	0.35	0.21
7	0.21	**0.74**	0.05	0.15	**0.72**	0.17
8	0.50	**0.59**	0.20	0.48	**0.57**	0.28
9	0.19	**0.85**	0.21	0.21	**0.87**	0.15
10	0.23	**0.76**	0.32	0.31	**0.82**	0.20
11	0.21	**0.73**	0.39	0.38	**0.77**	0.18
12	0.27	**0.52**	**0.62**	0.40	**0.62**	0.43
13	0.37	0.37	**0.75**	0.47	0.39	**0.71**
14	0.42	0.34	**0.73**	0.51	0.39	**0.70**
15	0.41	0.13	**0.58**	**0.61**	0.25	0.38
16	**0.60**	0.22	**0.65**	**0.75**	0.35	0.44

TABLE 3.13: CSUQ factor analyses by product. *(continued on pg. 70)*

Item	Amazon			Gmail		
	SysUse	InfoQual	IntQual	SysUse	InfoQual	IntQual
1	**0.70**	0.33	0.47	**0.70**	0.30	0.52
2	**0.77**	0.30	0.48	**0.81**	0.34	0.29
3	**0.74**	0.36	0.37	**0.71**	0.42	0.37
4	**0.52**	0.22	0.75	**0.76**	0.35	0.28
5	**0.61**	0.25	0.63	**0.83**	0.35	0.25
6	**0.71**	0.32	0.41	**0.69**	0.39	0.41
7	0.10	**0.69**	0.30	0.33	**0.73**	0.24
8	0.36	**0.73**	0.32	0.45	**0.67**	0.34
9	0.22	**0.83**	0.18	0.25	**0.86**	0.24
10	0.41	**0.68**	0.32	0.34	**0.78**	0.33
11	0.53	**0.65**	0.19	0.37	**0.75**	0.32
12	**0.54**	**0.56**	0.39	0.43	**0.56**	**0.49**
13	**0.49**	**0.46**	**0.54**	0.28	0.31	**0.85**
14	0.40	0.47	**0.65**	0.36	0.36	**0.79**
15	0.32	0.32	**0.72**	0.40	0.30	**0.58**
16	0.38	0.41	**0.77**	0.57	0.36	**0.56**

TABLE 3.13: CSUQ factor analyses by product. *(continued from pg. 69)*

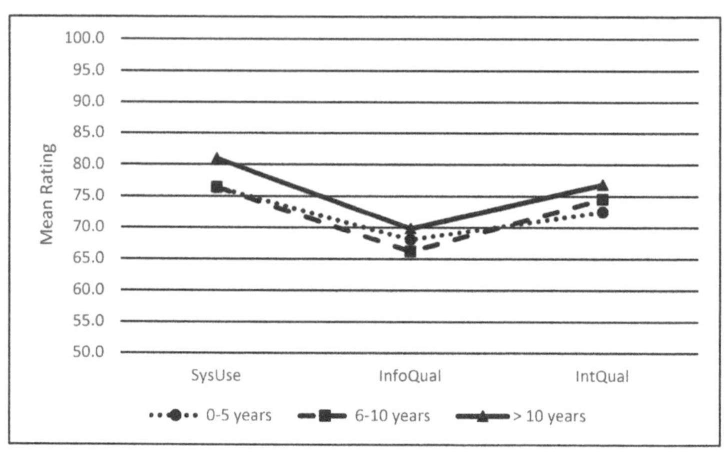

FIGURE 3.5: Interaction between years of product use and CSUQ subscale.

Frequency of use. The main effect of the frequency of use of the product was statistically significant (F(3, 1420) = 20.5, p < 0.0001), as was its interaction with Subscale (F(6, 2840) = 5.6, p < 0.0001; see Figure 3.6) and the three-way interaction with Subscale and Product (F(18, 2840) = 1.9, p = 0.014). Its interaction with Product was marginally significant (9, 1420) = 1.64, p = 0.099. The mean for usage more than once per day was 78.2 (B+), about once a day was 74.8 (B), about once a week was 69.3 (C), and less often than once a week was 63.4 (C-).

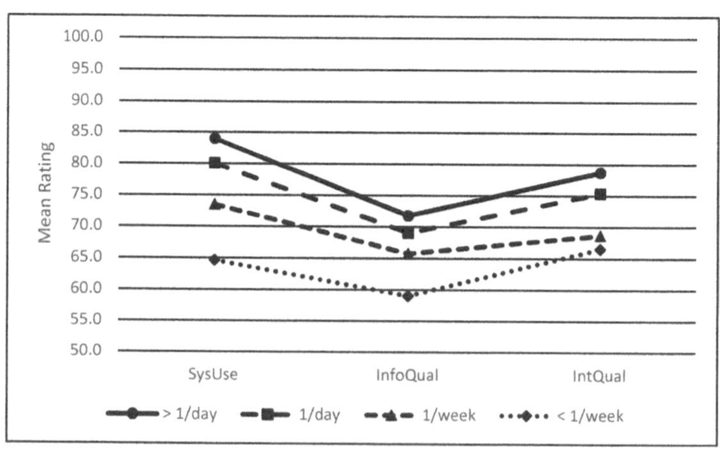

FIGURE 3.6: Interaction between frequency of product use and CSUQ subscale.

Comparison with SUS means from Kortum and Bangor (2013)

Given the differences of time and respondent populations between this study and the findings reported by Kortum and Bangor (2013), there was no expectation that the results would match exactly. Table 3.14 and Figure 3.7 illustrate the similarities and differences in the mean ratings between the studies for Excel, Word, Amazon, and Gmail. Table 3.15 shows the corresponding CGS grades (see Table 3.1) for the values in Table 3.14.

Comparisons of means across studies for each product indicated statistically significant differences for Excel ($t(674) = 10.6$, $p < 0.0001$), Amazon ($t(515) = 2.6$, $p = 0.01$), and Gmail ($t(390) = -3.8$, $p = 0.00015$), but not for Word ($t(679) = -0.6$, $p = 0.52$). When sample sizes are large, however, it is important to consider practical as well as statistical significance (Sauro & Lewis, 2016).

The CGS grades shown in Table 3.15 provide a method for assessing practical significance. As expected given no significant difference in SUS means despite the sample sizes, the assigned grade for Word (B) was the same for the means in both studies. For Amazon and Gmail the difference between the means was a partial grade step (Amazon: A+ vs. A; Gmail: B+ vs. A). The difference between the studies for Excel was one full grade step (C vs. D). Converting these grades to their numeric values as given in Table 3.1 for computing GPA (Amazon: 4.0 vs 4.0; Gmail: 3.7 vs. 4.0; Word: 3.0 vs. 3.0; Excel: 2.0 vs. 1.0), the mean GPA for this study was 3.175 and for Kortum & Bangor (2013) was 3.0, a mean difference of 0.175.

The mean SUS across products was 77.0 in the this study; in Kortum and Bangor (2013) it was 74.5. Both of these corresponded to a CGS grade of B.

Mean SUS	Excel	Word	Amazon	Gmail
Upper (this study)	72.5	77.4	86.8	80.5
Mean (this study)	**69.6**	**75.5**	**84.8**	**78.0**
Lower (this study)	66.7	73.5	82.7	75.5
Upper (K&B 2013)	57.7	77.1	82.8	84.8
Mean (K&B 2013)	**56.5**	**76.2**	**81.8**	**83.5**
Lower (K&B 2013)	55.3	75.3	80.8	82.2

TABLE 3.14: SUS means and 95% confidence intervals for SUS ratings.

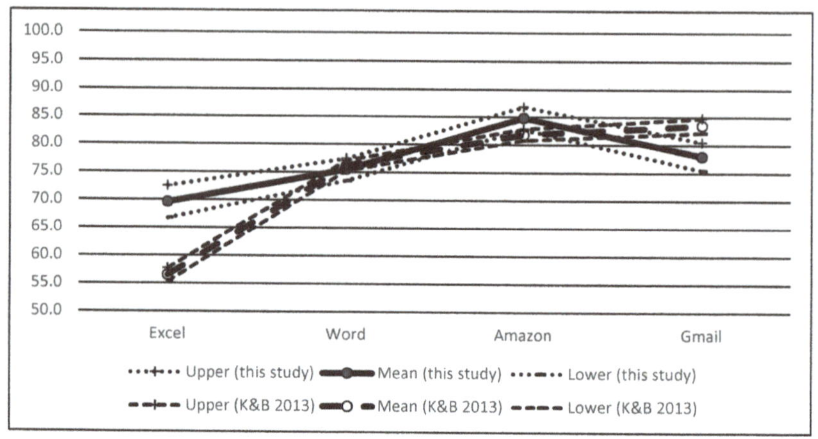

FIGURE 3.7: Comparison with K&B 2013 means including 95% confidence intervals.

CGS Grade	Excel	Word	Amazon	Gmail
Upper (this study)	C+	B+	A+	A-
Mean (this study)	C	B	A+	B+
Lower (this study)	C	B-	A	B
Upper (K&B 2013)	D	B	A	A+
Mean (K&B 2013)	D	B	A	A
Lower (K&B 2013)	D	B	A	A

TABLE 3.15: CGS grades for SUS means including 95% confidence intervals.

Correspondence between concurrently collected CSUQ and SUS means

Overall, the mean SUS was 76.5 and the mean CSUQ was 74.3. Although this difference was statistically significant (t(1436) = 7.6, p < 0.0001; 95% confidence interval around the absolute difference ranged from 1.6 to 2.7 points on a 0-100-point scale), both means were in the CGS's B range, which indicates little to no practical difference. The differences by product were:

- Excel: Mean SUS = 69.6 (C); mean CSUQ = 68.7 (C); t(389) = 1.6, p = 0.10

- Word: Mean SUS = 75.5 (B); mean CSUQ = 72.8 (B-); t(453) = 5.0, p < 0.0001

- Amazon: Mean SUS = 84.8 (A+); mean CSUQ = 82.3 (A); t(337) = 4.6, p < 0.0001

- Gmail: Mean SUS = 78.0 (B+); mean CSUQ = 75.3 (B); t(255) = 4.2, p < 0.0001

For one product, Excel, the mean SUS and CSUQ scores differed by less than one point and resolved to the same CGS grade of C. For the other three products, the CSUQ mean was about 2.5 points below the SUS means, but this difference never led to more than a fractional difference in associated CGS grade levels. In the CGS, a 2.5-point difference will often be in the same grade range, would never cross a full grade boundary, and would rarely cross more than one fractional grade boundary.

Discussion

Replication of Previous Psychometric Findings

Once again, the psychometric data were consistent with previous research, including acceptable levels of reliability, concurrent validity, construct validity, and sensitivity. Thus, over 30 years of research (1989-2019) have confirmed the psychometric quality of the PSSUQ/CSUQ as a measure of perceived usability.

Benchmarks for Everyday Products: Comparison with Kortum & Bangor (2013)

Despite the differences between this study and that of Kortum and Bangor (2013), the results were reasonably consistent. The absolute differences between the mean SUS scores across studies were relatively small except for Excel (about a 13-point difference). Analysis of the frequency of use for the IBM respondents in this study suggests the possibility that this difference may be due to relatively high usage, with more than half of the respondents indicating the use of Excel more frequently than once per day. Given the difference in time between this study and Kortum and Bangor (2013), of course, there may have been other factors affecting the differences such as the version of the product, but this finding supports the recommendation that researchers should collect and report information about the frequency of use when conducting benchmarking studies.

Grades assigned to SUS means using the Sauro-Lewis CGS (Table 1) were the same for Word, one fractional grade level for Amazon and Gmail, and one full grade levels for Excel. Averaging across products, the mean GPA deviation between the current study (3.175) and Kortum and Bangor (3.0) was 0.175 – on average, less than two-tenths of a grade level.

Correspondence between the SUS and the CSUQ

After conversion to a common 0-100-point scale, both overall means and means by product indicated a high degree of correspondence between the CSUQ and the SUS. This was the case both for their mean scores and, even more striking, after conversion to grades using the Sauro-Lewis curved grading scale. These findings add to the growing body of evidence supporting the interpretation of CSUQ scores using the curved grading scale originally developed for the SUS.

META-ANALYSIS OF CORRESPONDENCE BETWEEN THE SUS AND THE CSUQ

Table 3.16 shows the results of the studies conducted to date in which there was concurrent collection of CSUQ and SUS ratings of the same system or product.

Product/ System (Study)	SUS Mean	CSUQ Mean	Mean Differ- ence	SUS CGS	CSUQ CGS	SUS GPA	CSUQ GPA	GPA Differ- ence
Mind Maps (Berkman & Karahoca, 2016)	79.5	80.0	-0.5	A-	A-	4.0	4.0	0.0
Windows OS (Lewis, 2018b)	66.9	64.1	2.8	C	C-	2.0	1.7	0.3
Apple OS (Lewis, 2018b)	76.8	76.6	0.2	B	B	3.0	3.0	0.0
Excel (Lewis, 2018c)	69.6	68.7	0.9	C	C	2.0	2.0	0.0
Word (Lewis, 2018c)	75.5	72.8	2.7	B	B-	3.0	2.7	0.3

(continued on pg. 76)

Product/ System (Study)	SUS Mean	CSUQ Mean	Mean Difference	SUS CGS	CSUQ CGS	SUS GPA	CSUQ GPA	GPA Difference
Amazon (Lewis, 2018c)	84.8	82.3	2.5	A+	A	4.0	4.0	0.0
Gmail (Lewis, 2018c)	78.0	75.3	2.7	B+	B	3.3	3.0	0.3
Mean			1.6					0.1
Std Deviation			1.39					0.16
n			7					7
Std Error			0.52					0.06
df			6					6
Critical t (95% CI)			2.45					2.45
Critical d (95% CI)			1.28					0.15
Upper bound			2.90					0.28
Lower bound			0.33					-0.02

TABLE 3.16: Correspondence between SUS and CSUQ means and grade point averages.

Across the studies, the mean of the difference scores was 1.6, with a 95% confidence interval ranging from 0.3 to 2.9. This indicates that it is very unlikely that the true difference between the questionnaires' means is less than 0.3 or more than 2.9, and is more likely about one-and-a-half points on a scale that ranges from 0 to 100. After translation to a grade point value based on the Sauro-Lewis curved grading scale and using a standard assignment of numerical values to grades, the mean difference in GPA was 0.1, with a 95% confidence interval ranging from -0.02 to 0.28. This means that it is plausible based on the available evidence that con-currently collected SUS and CSUQ scores produce identical mean GPAs.

- The only language for which the CSUQ has been formally translated with psychometric qualification is the Turkish version (T-CSUQ).

- The results of the four studies discussed in this chapter all provided evidence of acceptable levels of psychometric properties for the CSUQ consistent with the initial research provided in Chapter 2, including reliability, concurrent validity, construct validity, and sensitivity.

- The key to current interpretation of PSSUQ and CSUQ means is through the use of open-source norms initially developed for the SUS.

- The basis for this practice is data from three recently conducted studies in which participants rated systems and products with both the CSUQ and the SUS, finding close correspondence on average across a range of products and systems, especially after conversion to grade point averages based on the Sauro-Lewis curved grading scale for the SUS.

- Researchers should collect and report information about the frequency of use when conducting benchmarking studies.

## CHAPTER 4

USING THE PSSUQ AND CSUQ: BASIC ANALYSES

The focus of the next two chapters is how to actually use the questionnaires. The most common basic statistical tasks with these types of data are estimation, comparison with a benchmark, and comparison of two sets of data (independent or dependent), which are the topics of this chapter. The next chapter will cover more advanced types of analyses (analysis of variance, multiple comparisons, and multiple regression).

For more background on quantitative analysis of user experience metrics, see *Quantifying the User Experience* (Sauro & Lewis, 2016) and the *Excel and R Companion to the 2nd Edition of Quantifying the User Experience* (Lewis & Sauro, 2016). I can't cover all of the material in those books in Chapters 4 and 5, so I'm going to present the methods I usually use without a bunch of explanation (and without the supporting math). To as great an extent as possible I'll use Excel and online calculators for the examples in Chapter 4, but for the more complex analyses in Chapter 5 I'll demonstrate analysis with two major statistical software packages: SPSS (popular monthly subscription product) and R (popular free open source product).

 **TIP:**

This is a book about how to use a standardized questionnaire, which means you will be more successful using it if you have some quantitative skills, even if you wind up using online calculators for your analyses. If you don't have these skills, hopefully there's someone on your team who does. If not, then I strongly recommend that you pick up a book like *Quantifying the User Experience* (Sauro & Lewis, 2016). If you need professional quantitative assistance, consider reaching out to a company like MeasuringU for a quote.

The usual way of estimating the central tendency of a set of data is with the arithmetic mean – add up the scores and divide by the number of scores. This is a good start, but it doesn't take the variability of measurement into account, so you don't know how precise the estimate is. To overcome that limitation, you should compute a confidence interval, which establishes a range of plausibility for the estimate by adding and subtracting an amount that is affected by (1) the variability of the data (the standard deviation), (2) the sample size, and (3) the desired level of confidence. There are times when you might not want to be consistent with statistical conventions regarding the level of confidence (see Sauro & Lewis, 2016, Chapter 9), but in this book I'm going to stick with the estimation convention of using 95% confidence intervals and the statistical testing convention of setting the acceptable level of a Type I error (p) to less than 0.05 (this will be covered in a little more detail below).

Estimation: Example 1

The data in Table 4.1 came from a usability study of the CrossPad (see Figure 4.1) from around the year 2000. The CrossPad was a device that captured a user's handwriting as the user wrote on standard note paper. To do this, the tablet had an array of sensors in the area under the paper and the pen had a small radio transmitter activated by a tip switch closed by the pressure of writing. It was designed to appeal to users who were comfortable working with a pen and paper notepad, but who needed electronic storage of their notes (handwriting and drawings), conveniently captured during the normal process of note taking. The expected user population were professionals who took notes as they consulted with clients (for example, architects) or who were unable to take laptop computers into certain environments (for example, lawyers taking notes in a courtroom).

Software bundled with the CrossPad had some capability for unconstrained handwriting recognition, but the primary purpose of the software was the ability to file the electronic copies of the handwritten pages (with optional keywords) into electronic notebooks for later retrieval. Users could create, rename, and delete notebook names, with the list of valid notebook names synchronized when users connected the pad to a computer to upload pages of notes. These features were in support of a user requirement to allow the assignment of pages to notebooks as users took notes on the pad. After completing these types of tasks, the six participants in the usability study completed the PSSUQ. This study used Version 2 of the PSSUQ because it predated the development of Version 3, so to keep the analysis current, the table shows ratings only from the 16 items that make up Version 3 of the PSSUQ, along with estimation of 95% confidence intervals for each of the items.

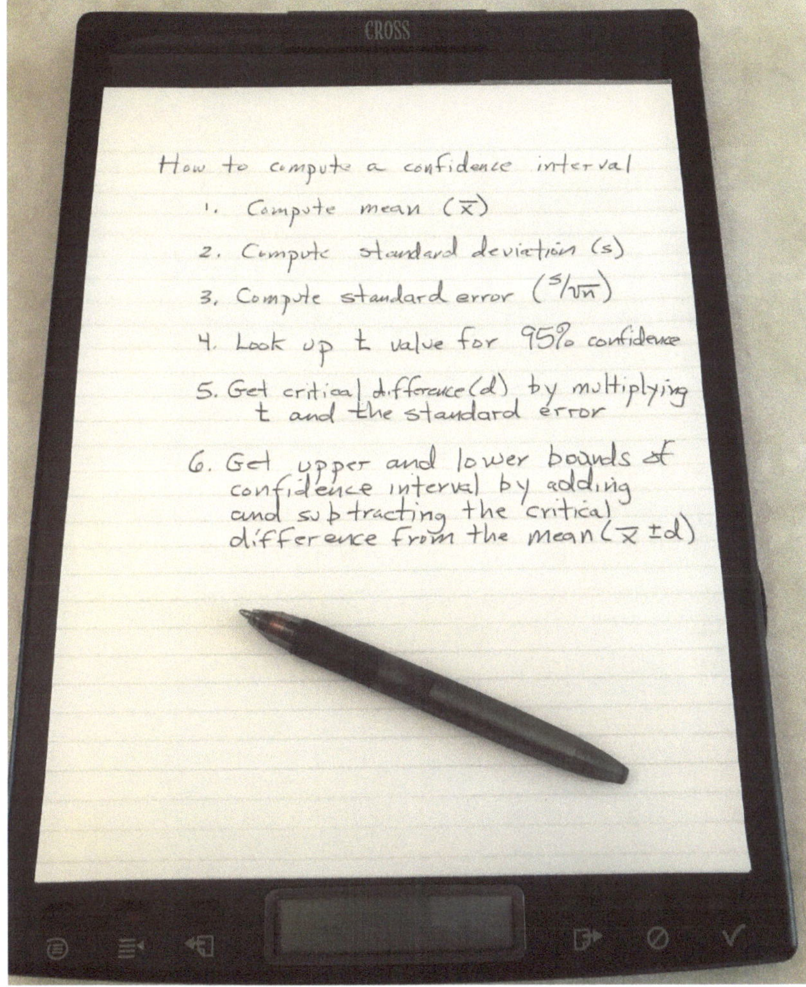

FIGURE 4.1: The CrossPad (with notes about computing confidence intervals).

Participant	1	2	3	4	5	6	7	8	9	10	11	12	13	14	15	16
1	1.0	1.0	1.0	1.0	1.0	1.0	1.0	1.0	1.0	2.0	1.0	1.0	1.0	1.0	2.0	1.0
2	1.0	1.0	2.0	1.0	1.0	1.0	3.0	2.0	2.0	3.0	2.0	1.0	1.0	1.0	1.0	1.0
3	2.0	2.0	2.0	2.0	1.0	2.0	4.0	3.0	3.0	3.0	2.0	2.0	2.0	2.0	2.0	2.0
4	2.0	1.0	1.0	1.0	2.0	1.0	.	1.0	2.0	2.0	2.0	3.0	1.0	1.0	2.0	1.0
5	3.0	3.0	2.0	3.0	2.0	2.0	6.0	5.0	3.0	2.0	3.0	3.0	1.0	2.0	4.0	4.0
6	2.0	1.0	1.0	.	.	.	1.0	1.0	1.0	1.0	1.0	1.0	1.0	1.0	1.0	1.0
Mean	1.83	1.50	1.50	1.60	1.40	1.40	3.00	2.17	2.00	2.17	1.83	1.83	1.17	1.33	2.00	1.67
Std Dev	0.75	0.84	0.55	0.89	0.55	0.55	2.12	1.60	0.89	0.75	0.75	0.98	0.41	0.52	1.10	1.21
n	6	6	6	5	5	5	5	6	6	6	6	6	6	6	6	6
Std Error	0.31	0.34	0.22	0.40	0.24	0.24	0.95	0.65	0.37	0.31	0.31	0.40	0.17	0.21	0.45	0.49
df	5	5	5	4	4	4	4	5	5	5	5	5	5	5	5	5
t(95)	2.57	2.57	2.57	2.78	2.78	2.78	2.78	2.57	2.57	2.57	2.57	2.57	2.57	2.57	2.57	2.57
d(95)	0.79	0.88	0.57	1.11	0.68	0.68	2.63	1.68	0.94	0.79	0.79	1.03	0.43	0.54	1.15	1.27
95% Upper	2.62	2.38	2.07	2.71	2.08	2.08	5.63	3.85	2.94	2.96	2.62	2.87	1.60	1.88	3.15	2.94
95% Lower	1.04	0.62	0.93	0.49	0.72	0.72	0.37	0.49	1.06	1.38	1.04	0.80	0.74	0.79	0.85	0.40

TABLE 4.1: PSSUQ ratings from usability study of the CrossPad (circa 2000).

Let's take a look at Table 4.1, copied from an Excel spreadsheet. The data are arranged in rows, with one case per row, where a "case" is the data obtained with a participant. A dot (.) in a cell indicates the participant did not rate that item. The Excel formulas used for each computational step were:

- Mean: =average(listOfCells)
- Standard Deviation: =StDev(listOfCells)
- n: =count(listOfCells)
- Standard Error: =StdDev/sqrt(n)
- df: =n-1
- t(95): =tinv(.05,df)
- d(95): =StdError*t(95)
- 95% Upper: =Mean+d(95)
- 95% Lower: =Mean-d(95)

To recap, you start by computing the mean with Excel's =average function, the standard deviation with the =stdev function, and the sample size (n) with the =count function. The standard error is the standard deviation divided by the square root of the sample size. To get the critical value of t for a 95% confidence interval, you need to know what values to use in the =tinv function, which are 0.05 (1 − 0.95) for "probability" and n-1 for "degrees of freedom" (again, for background, see Sauro & Lewis, 2016). Compute the critical difference for the confidence interval by multiplying the obtained values of t and the standard error, then get the upper and lower bounds of the confidence interval by adding and subtracting this critical difference to/from the mean.

Setting this up in Excel or a professional analysis program like SPSS makes sense if you're going to run the same analysis on multiple sets of data, such as all 16 PSSUQ items as shown in Table 4.1. If you only need to run one analysis, then an online calculator might be all you need, and for people who aren't familiar with statistics or are not comfortable using functions in Excel, this can be very helpful.

For example, there is a confidence interval calculator at https://measuringu.com/ci-calc/. To check it out, let's see if we get the same confidence interval for the first PSSUQ item with the calculator that we did in Excel. Figure 4.2 shows a screen shot of the results, which shows the same values as those shown in Table 4.1 for the sample size, mean, standard deviation, standard error, and upper and lower limits of the 95% confidence interval.

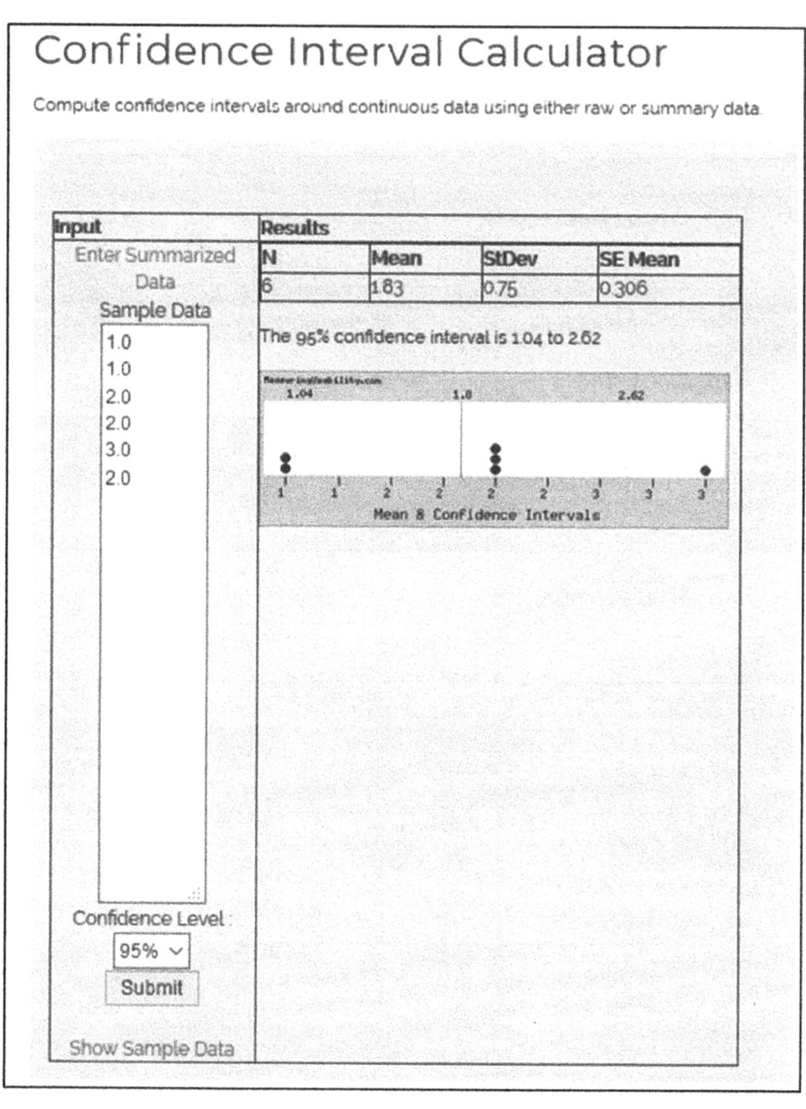

FIGURE 4.2: Analyzing PSSUQ Item 1 with the MeasuringU confidence interval calculator.

> When using the confidence interval calculator, because it counts all of the lines you enter even if they are blank, make sure the value of N matches your sample size.

I usually don't spend a lot of time analyzing PSSUQ data at the item level, but it's interesting to note that the rating for Item 7 ("The system gave error messages that clearly told me how to fix problems") received the highest (poorest) rating (3.00) – a common normative pattern mentioned in Chapter 2.

But what about the overall PSSUQ and its subscales? Table 4.2 shows means and 95% confidence intervals computed from the data in Table 4.1 for SysUse, InfoQual, IntQual, PSSUQ, and PSSUQ100 (overall PSSUQ converted to a 0-100-point scale suitable for comparison with SUS curved grading scale norms – see Chapter 3).

Participant	SysUse	InfoQual	IntQual	PSSUQ	PSSUQ100
1	1.00	1.17	1.33	1.13	97.9
2	1.17	2.17	1.00	1.50	91.7
3	1.83	2.83	2.00	2.25	79.2
4	1.33	2.00	1.33	1.53	91.1
5	2.50	3.67	2.33	3.00	66.7
6	1.33	1.00	1.00	1.08	98.7
Mean	1.53	2.14	1.50	1.75	87.54
Std Dev	0.55	1.01	0.55	0.74	12.40
n	6	6	6	6	6
Std Error	0.23	0.41	0.22	0.30	5.06
df	5	5	5	5	5
t(95)	2.57	2.57	2.57	2.57	2.57
d(95)	0.58	1.06	0.57	0.78	13.01
95% Upper	2.11	3.20	2.07	2.53	100.55
95% Lower	0.95	1.08	0.93	0.97	74.53

TABLE 4.2: Overall PSSUQ and subscales from usability study of the CrossPad (circa 2000).

What can we do with just one set of results? For one thing, note that, consistent with the normative pattern discussed in Chapter 2, the InfoQual mean was a bit larger than the other subscales, as expected. More importantly, when converted to a grade using the rubric in Table 3.1, a PSSUQ100 mean of 87.54 corresponds to an A+, and the lower and upper limits of the 95% confidence interval correspond to grades of B and A+. This means that even with the small sample size of 6, the data show that this user group, when completing this task set with this product, had a pretty high opinion of its usability. The average rating was an A+, and the 95% confidence interval indicates it is unlikely that if the experiment were conducted again, the mean would be lower than a B.

Estimation: Example 2

The outcome in the previous example is a pretty good result, but that wasn't the first iteration of usability testing with the product. Tables 4.3 and 4.4 show the results from the first iteration, conducted with four participants.

Participant	SysUse	InfoQual	IntQual	PSSUQ	PSSUQ100
1	1.83	2.50	2.00	2.13	81.3
2	2.50	3.33	3.67	3.13	64.6
3	3.17	6.17	1.00	4.13	47.8
4	2.33	3.33	3.00	2.88	68.8
Mean	2.46	3.83	2.42	3.06	65.59
Std Dev	0.55	1.60	1.17	0.83	13.83
n	4	4	4	4	4
Std Error	0.28	0.80	0.58	0.41	6.91
df	3	3	3	3	3
t(95)	3.18	3.18	3.18	3.18	3.18
d(95)	0.88	2.55	1.86	1.32	22.00
95% Upper	3.33	6.39	4.27	4.38	87.59
95% Lower	1.58	1.28	0.56	1.74	43.59

TABLE 4.3: Overall PSSUQ and subscales from first usability study of the CrossPad (circa 2000).

The results didn't seem to be as good in this evaluation, with a mean PSSUQ100 of 65.59 (C) and a lower limit of the confidence interval of 43.59 (F). Granted, the upper limit was 87.59 (A+), but with only four participants we don't get terribly precise measurement, evidenced by the 95% confidence interval covering 44.0 points (43.59 – 87.59) and a grade range from F to A+. Contrast this with the first example, in which the confidence interval had a length of 26.0 points and a grade range from B to A+ -- quite a bit more precision even though the sample size was just six participants (but still not terribly precise because there were just six participants).

Examination of these estimates is not equivalent to a formal statistical test of the data from these two studies – we'll get to that in the following section on comparison of two independent sets of data. We couldn't publish these estimation findings in a scientific journal, but for practical industrial research the results were promising. The changes made to the product based on the objective findings (task times, completion rates, prioritized problem descriptions) from the first evaluation with four participants appeared to have improved the perceived user experience in the second iteration.

COMPARISON WITH A BENCHMARK

When working with quantitative user experience questionnaires such as the PSSUQ, the curved grading scale (Table 3.1) provides guidance on setting quantitative benchmarks, either for mean scores or grade point averages. Because we are moving from estimation to formal statistical testing, let's start with a quick review of how formal statistical testing works.

TIP:

> If you're interested in more details about UX benchmarking, be sure to take a look at *Benchmarking the User Experience* (Sauro, 2018).

Quick Review of Formal Statistical Testing

In a parody article published in Omni magazine, Searles (1978, p. 110) defined "p" as "the world's most specific way of saying 'maybe'." The article was humorous, but that statement was true. The value of p, computed from one or more sets of data, indicates the likelihood that an

Participant	1	2	3	4	5	6	7	8	9	10	11	12	13	14	15	16
1	2.0	2.0	2.0	2.0	2.0	1.0	3.0	2.0	2.0	3.0	3.0	2.0	2.0	2.0	2.0	2.0
2	3.0	3.0	2.0	2.0	2.0	3.0	4.0	4.0	3.0	3.0	2.0	4.0	3.0	4.0	4.0	4.0
3	2.0	3.0	5.0	4.0	4.0	1.0	7.0	7.0	7.0	6.0	6.0	4.0	1.0	1.0	.	4.0
4	2.0	2.0	3.0	2.0	2.0	3.0	4.0	4.0	3.0	3.0	3.0	3.0	3.0	3.0	3.0	3.0
Mean	2.25	2.50	3.00	2.50	2.50	2.00	4.50	4.25	3.75	3.75	3.50	3.25	2.25	2.50	3.00	3.25
Std Dev	0.50	0.58	1.41	1.00	1.00	1.15	1.73	2.06	2.22	1.50	1.73	0.96	0.96	1.29	1.00	0.96
n	4	4	4	4	4	4	4	4	4	4	4	4	4	4	3	4
Std Error	0.25	0.29	0.71	0.50	0.50	0.58	0.87	1.03	1.11	0.75	0.87	0.48	0.48	0.65	0.58	0.48
df	3	3	3	3	3	3	3	3	3	3	3	3	3	3	2	3
t(95)	3.18	3.18	3.18	3.18	3.18	3.18	3.18	3.18	3.18	3.18	3.18	3.18	3.18	3.18	4.30	3.18
d(95)	0.80	0.92	2.25	1.59	1.59	1.84	2.76	3.28	3.53	2.39	2.76	1.52	1.52	2.05	2.48	1.52
95% Upper	3.05	3.42	5.25	4.09	4.09	3.84	7.26	7.53	7.28	6.14	6.26	4.77	3.77	4.55	5.48	4.77
95% Lower	1.45	1.58	0.75	0.91	0.91	0.16	1.74	0.97	0.22	1.36	0.74	1.73	0.73	0.45	0.52	1.73

TABLE 4.4: PSSUQ ratings from first usability study of the CrossPad (circa 2000).

observed difference would happen if there was actually no real difference (technically known as a Type I error – deciding an observed effect is real when it really isn't). As mentioned earlier in this chapter, the convention for deciding that a particular outcome is unlikely enough to support acting as if the effect is real is p < 0.05.

This means that in the long run, we are willing to be wrong one out of every 20 statistical tests, believing there is a statistically significant difference when there really isn't. Note that this error rate applies to tests conducted when there is no difference – when there is a difference the focus shifts to the Type II error – the likelihood of failing to discover a difference when one does exist. The thing is, you never know in advance whether there is or isn't a difference – making this an exact way of saying maybe. The good news is that even though the use of formal statistical testing does not guarantee 100% correct decisions, it doesn't have to be perfect to be useful.

Table 4.5 shows the four possible outcomes of a formal statistical test.

Decision	Reality	
	Ho is true	Ho is false
Evidence is NOT strong enough to reject Ho (p > α)	Correctly failed to reject Ho	Made Type II error
Evidence IS strong enough to reject Ho (p < α)	Made Type I error	Correctly rejected Ho

TABLE 4.5: The four outcomes of formal statistical testing.

Let's break down Table 4.5. First, it's important to understand Ho – also known as the null hypothesis. It seems counterintuitive, but the strategy of formal statistical testing is to start by assuming there is no real difference. This assumption of "no difference" is the null hypothesis (Ho). After you collect data, either to compare the mean of observed data with a fixed benchmark or the comparison of means, the statistical test assesses the likelihood of getting that data if there is actually no difference. If that likelihood is low (conventionally p < 0.05), then you reject Ho. If likelihood is higher, you fail to reject Ho.

Note that when the data are not convincing, the decision is to "fail to reject Ho", not to "accept Ho." This is an important distinction because there are at least two reasons for failing to reject Ho. One possibility is that there really is no difference, but the other is that there is a difference but a combination of high variability and low sample size caused the test to be nonsignificant. In other words, if the data strongly indicate a significant difference, you reject Ho, but if the data are not compelling, you refrain from making any claim.

Returning to Table 4.5, the four outcomes are the possible states that flow from the binary decision (reject or fail to reject Ho) and the binary state of reality (Ho is true, there is no difference, or Ho is false, there is a difference). If Ho is true and the evidence for a difference is weak, then you have correctly failed to reject Ho. If the evidence is strong and Ho is false, then you have correctly rejected Ho. Those are the two ways to be right.

There are also two ways to be wrong. If the reality is that Ho is true, there really is no difference, but the data appear to be strong enough to reject Ho, then a Type I error has occurred (deciding there's a difference when there really isn't one). If the reality is that Ho is false, there really is a difference, but the data are not strong enough to be convincing, then a Type II error has occurred (deciding there's not a difference when there really is).

The focus of scientific statistical testing is the control of the Type I error because the perceived damage of a Type I error, which would result in publishing findings that are not true, is generally considered to be more damaging than a Type II error, which would delay the publication of findings until, if ever, sufficient evidence is found to support publication. In industrial testing, it is possible that Type II errors could be equally or more damaging to the enterprise than Type I errors, in which case it would be reasonable to set a to ▯ value higher than 0.05 (for example, 0.10 or 0.20). Without justification for using a nonstandard significance criterion, however, the best practice is to use 0.05.

There is one more topic that we need to cover before moving on to the benchmark comparison examples. The default in statistical testing is to conduct two-tailed tests. This terminology comes from the depiction of the rejection regions in the distribution of differences. As shown in Figure 4.3a, a two-tailed test has (typically equal) rejection regions in each tail of the distribution, so it is possible to reject Ho without regard to whether the observed difference is positive or negative. This is the right way to set up the test when you don't know in advance which way the data will go.

When you're comparing data with a benchmark, however, you usually only care whether you have compelling evidence that you've reached or exceeded the benchmark. In that case, it's OK to use a one-tailed test. The advantage of a one-tailed test over a two-tailed test is that the criterion for declaring statistical significance is a bit lower (easier to achieve). In Figure 4.3a, the 0.05 for alpha has been distributed evenly between the tails, so for the depicted z test, you would declare a significance whether the test statistic was z < -1.96 or z > +1.96. In Figure 4.3b, the 0.05 for alpha is all in the right tail, so you could declare statistical significance when z > + 1.65 (slightly less than 1.96, but no matter how negative the outcome might be, you could not claim significance).

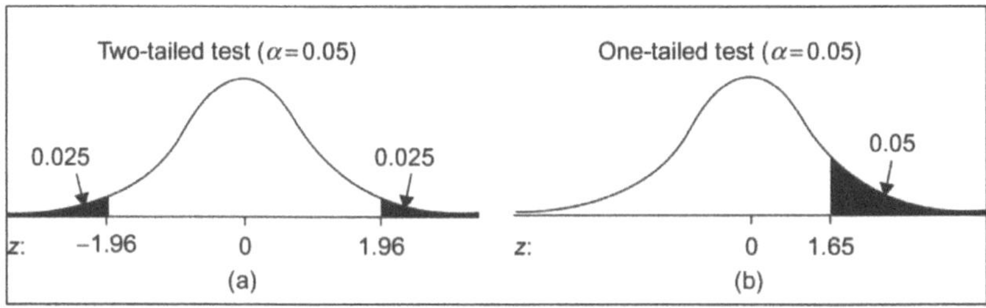

FIGURE 4.3: Depiction of two-tailed and one-tailed rejection regions for statistical testing.

Figure 4.3 uses a z test as an example because it is one of the simplest tests. Without getting too technical, a z score is a measure of the number of standard deviations between two points (e.g., a mean and a benchmark, or two means). For normal distributions, a distance of plus or minus two standard deviations around a mean difference covers 95% of the distribution, leaving 2.5% in each tail. To get exactly 95%, it's plus or minus 1.96 standard deviations. For a one-tailed test (Figure 4.3b), if you start from the farthest point of the left tail and keep going until you cover 95% of the distribution, the z score where you stop would be 1.65, leaving 5% in the right tail for the rejection region.

Because we'll often be working with relatively small sample sizes, the examples will use a variation of the z test known as the t test. There is only one z distribution, but there is a family of t distributions where each member of the family is defined by its degrees of freedom (df). That's why the convention for reporting the results of t tests includes the df, for example, $t(9) = 2.3$, $p = 0.012$. The number inside parentheses is the df, and I computed the value of p using the Excel function =TTEST which requires three inputs – the value of t, the df, and the number of tails in the test. The rules for computing df are different for different types of tests.

OK, back to the examples …

Comparison with Benchmark: Example 1

Table 3.1, the Sauro-Lewis curved grading scale for the SUS, is an excellent resource to use to justify a target for the SUS or any of the questionnaires that have been shown to produce comparable scores, such as the UMUX-LITE or PSSUQ/CSUQ. A common industrial benchmark is a score of 80, which is easy to remember and is close to the boundary between A- and A in the curved grading scale. From Table 4.2, the mean PSSUQ100 was 87.54 with a standard deviation of 12.4 and a sample size of 6. 87.54 is higher than 80, but is this sufficient evidence to support a claim that the mean of 87.54 is statistically significantly better than 80?

To run the test with this information, we'll conduct a one-tailed t test. Because we're testing the hypothesis that the observed mean is higher than the benchmark, we compute t by:

- Subtracting the benchmark from the observed mean (87.54 - 80 = 7.54)

- Computing the standard error by dividing the standard deviation by the square root of the sample size (12.4/2.449 = 5.06)

- Computing t by dividing the result of the first step by the result of the second step (7.54/5.06 = 1.49)

- Computing the df by subtracting one from the sample size (6 - 1 = 5)

- Using Excel to determine the probability of getting this result if there's really no difference between the mean and the benchmark (=TDIST(1.49,5,1) = 0.098)

Strictly speaking, the result of this test was that it was inconclusive (t(5) = 1.49, p = 0.098). A probability of 0.098 is fairly small, but it is not less than the conventional criterion of 0.05. On the other hand, the data came from a small-sample usability study typical of much industrial usability engineering practice. As a user experience practitioner not planning to publish these results, there are a number of things you could do with this outcome.

You might have already established a convention in your lab that for small-sample usability studies, the appropriate criterion for statistical control of the Type I error would be to use 0.10 or 0.15 instead of the stricter (but more prone to Type II errors) convention of $p < 0.05$. In that case, you would have, for your research context, sufficient evidence to declare having surpassed the benchmark. Keep in mind that you should have established this practice before conducting the test, not after.

You could explore what happens if you relax your benchmark to something less than 80. For example, in Table 3.1 a 77 is close to the boundary between B and B+. Using that as the benchmark instead of 80, the test result would be t(5) = 2.08, p = 0.046. Because 0.046 is less than 0.05, you have a conventionally significant result, evidence that your observed mean of 87.54 is significantly higher than the benchmark of 77.

Rather than exploring what happens with a single relaxed benchmark, you could compute a one-tailed confidence interval around the mean of 87.54 with special emphasis on the value of the lower bound of the interval. For the previous estimation exercise, Table 4.2 showed a 95% confidence interval for PSSUQ100 that ranged from about 74.5 to 100, but that was a two-tailed interval – appropriate for estimation, but less appropriate for exploring the relationship between a mean and a benchmark.

The computation of the appropriate confidence interval is the same as that shown in Table 4.2 except for the critical value of t. In Table 4.2, that value was 2.57, computed in Excel using =TINV(0.05,5). To get the appropriate value for an otherwise identical one-tailed evaluation, double 0.05 to 0.10, which gives a critical t value of 2.01 (=TINV(0.10,5)). Now the critical value of d for the confidence interval is the standard error of 5.06 times 2.01, which is 10.17, and the one-sided 95% confidence interval is 87.54 ± 10.17, which ranges from 77.37 to 97.71. This interval has both lower and upper bounds, so how can it be a one-sided interval – and what kind of oxymoron is that? The answer is that we only care about one side of the interval, which in this case is the lower bound. What this tells us is that the data from this study, using the conventional rejection criterion of p < 0.05, would find a statistically significant difference for any benchmark lower than or equal to 77.37. Referring back to Table 3.1, we can be 95% confident that the results from the usability study would beat a criterion of 77.2, and thus, the user experience grade is at least a B+.

Comparison with Benchmark: Example 2

In the year 2000 we were just beginning to experiment with voice user interfaces (VUIs) with which customers could call companies and, instead of having to use touchtone to navigate a menu structure, use voice recognition to select options. Table 4.6 shows the PSSUQ overall and subscale ratings from an evaluation of a planned demo system for basic library, banking, and calendar functions.

Participant	SysUse	InfoQual	IntQual	PSSUQ	PSSUQ100
1	1.5	1.4	1.0	1.3	95.0
2	2.0	2.0	2.0	2.0	83.3
3	4.0	2.9	2.7	3.4	60.0
4	1.6	1.0	1.3	1.3	95.0
5	1.8	3.4	1.7	2.3	78.3
6	1.0	1.3	1.7	1.2	96.7
7	2.8	3.0	3.0	2.9	68.3
Mean	2.10	2.14	1.91	2.06	82.38
Std Dev	1.00	0.96	0.72	0.86	14.36
n	7	7	7	7	7
Std Error	0.38	0.36	0.27	0.33	5.43
df	6	6	6	6	6
t(90)	1.94	1.94	1.94	1.94	1.94
d(90)	0.74	0.70	0.53	0.63	10.55
90% Upper	4.04	4.09	3.86	4.00	84.32
90% Lower	1.36	1.44	1.39	1.42	71.83

t-test	1-tailed
Mean	82.38
Benchmark	71.1
Difference	11.28
Std Error	5.43
t	2.08
df	6
p	0.04

TABLE 4.6: PSSUQ ratings from voice interaction demo (circa 2000).

At the time we conducted this usability study, the curved grading scale in Table 3.1 did not exist. If it had existed, though, given how little experience we had with these types of designs in 2000, we could have reasonably set an initial benchmark to establish whether the user experience in the study was at least a little better than average. In Table 3.1, the lowest value for a C+ is 71.1, so that would have been a reasonable benchmark to use. As shown in the table, a 90% confidence interval for PSSUQ100 ranged from 71.83 to 84.32. As discussed above, a two-tailed 90% confidence interval produces the appropriate lower bound for a one-tailed 95% interval. For these data, because the lower bound was 71.83 (greater than the benchmark of 71.1), this indicates that this benchmark was exceeded in the study. For the formal statistical test, the outcome of the one-tailed t-test, shown at the bottom of the table, was statistically significant ($t(6) = 2.08$, $p = 0.04$).

COMPARISON OF TWO SETS OF DATA

Sometimes you might be less interested in how one set of data compares to a static benchmark, and be more interested in the comparison of two sets of data, for example, comparing your product with a competitor, or your current version with the new version under development. When there are two sets of PSSUQ (or any kind of) data, it makes a difference whether the data came from two different groups of participants (different people in each group) or were two ratings from the same group of participants (formally known as "dependent" data). Other common terms for this distinction are between-subjects (independent) and within-subjects (dependent) experimental designs. The different experimental designs have different strengths and weaknesses.

When you have the same person work with two different products, their first experience might influence their second experience (performance and/or perception), but you can reduce the magnitude of these carry-over effects by counterbalancing the order in which participants work with the products. Key advantages of a within-subjects design are (1) having experienced both, participants can indicate which product they preferred and (2) measurement variability is much lower so it is easier to achieve statistical significance with smaller sample sizes. Disadvantages of within-subjects designs are (1) it requires more time per participant to complete the study, increasing the likelihood of people not being able to finish in the available time and (2) both products have to be available at the same time.

Between-subjects designs have complementary advantages and disadvantages relative to within-subjects designs. When the assessment of two products is independent, the experiences of one group cannot influence the experiences of the other, but participants have no basis for comparing their experiences across products. It takes less time per participant to complete the study and the products do not have to be available at the same time, but you may need to acquire more participants to overcome the increase in measurement variability.

Comparison of Two Independent Sets of Data: Example 1

For this first example, let's return to the CrossPad data in Tables 4.2 and 4.4. For a formal statistical test of these data, Ho is the null hypothesis that there is no difference between the first and second iterations of usability testing. The data needed to conduct an independent-groups t-test are, for each set of data, the mean, the standard deviation, and the sample size. For this example, those PSSUQ100 values were:

- Iteration 1 (Table 4.3): Mean = 65.59, standard deviation = 13.83, n = 4

- Iteration 2 (Table 4.2): Mean = 87.54, standard deviation = 12.40, n = 6

There are different ways to compute the degrees of freedom for independent t-tests. The simplest is to add the sample sizes together and subtract two. In this example, that's 6 + 4 - 2 = 8.

 TIP:

When the variability of the groups is not equal, it may be necessary to use a different method to compute the degrees of freedom. Sauro and Lewis (2016) explain how to do this on p. 69 of the second edition of *Quantifying the User Experience*. Normally, however, you should be able to work with the simple formula $df = n_1 + n_2 - 2$.

Next, we need to compute the value of t, using these steps:

- Subtract one mean from the other to get the mean difference, typically subtracting the smaller mean from the larger (87.54 - 65.59 = 21.95).

- Start getting the standard error by first computing, for each group, the ratio of the square of the standard deviation by the sample size (Iteration 1: $13.83^2/4 = 47.82$, Iteration 2: $12.40^2/6 = 25.63$).

- Finish computing the standard error by adding those ratios together and taking their square root (=SQRT(47.82+25.63) = 8.57).

- Finally, compute t by dividing the mean difference by the standard error (21.95/8.57 = 2.56).

With t and df (and for this type of evaluation, using a two-tailed test), use Excel to find the likelihood of a difference this large if there was actually no improvement between iterations -- =TDIST(2.56,8,2) = 0.03. So the conclusion from the formal test is that the difference was statistically significant (t(8) = 2.56, p = 0.03).

You might wonder about the 95% confidence intervals from Tables 4.2 and 4.4, which substantially overlapped one another (Iteration 1: 43.6 - 87.6; Iteration 2: 74.5 - 100). If the confidence intervals overlap, how can the statistical test be significant?

This can happen because the standard error for the statistical test is the combination of the standard errors from both sets of data, as are the degrees of freedom. For example, the data used to compute the confidence interval for the first CrossPad usability study had only three degrees of freedom and, because the sample size was four, a fairly large standard error, so the resulting confidence interval was very wide. I usually include the confidence intervals for each group when I analyze this type of data because they illustrate the precision (or lack of precision) of measurement for each group.

To understand the relationship between the outcome of an independent-groups t-test and confidence, you can compute the confidence interval around the mean difference rather than around each mean. The values you need to do this are much the same as those used to perform the test of significance (mean difference: 21.95, df: 8, standard error: 8.57). Instead of computing a t-ratio, however, you need to determine the critical value of t for 95% confidence when df = 8, which you can do with the =TINV function in Excel: =TINV(.05,8) = 2.306. With these values in hand, the steps for computing the confidence interval are:

- Determine the critical difference by multiplying the critical value of t and the standard error (2.305 * 8.57 = 19.76).

- Compute the lower limit of the 95% confidence interval by subtracting the critical difference from the mean difference (21.95 - 19.76 = 2.19).

- Compute the upper limit of the 95% confidence interval by adding the critical difference to the mean difference (21.95 + 19.76 = 41.72).

So the 95% confidence interval around the mean difference of 21.95 ranged from 2.19 to 41.71. Note that this confidence interval does not include 0. Because a mean difference of 0 is the definition of the null hypothesis (Ho), when a confidence interval around a mean difference does not include 0, this is evidence that supports rejection of Ho, consistent with the test of significance. A test of significance provides a p-value which, if less than 0.05, is evidence sufficient to reject Ho.

A 95% confidence interval around a mean difference provides that same information when the interval excludes 0, but also shows the plausible range of mean differences given the available information. In this example, the observed mean difference was 21.95, which is pretty large for a scale that ranges from 0-100. The sample sizes in the usability studies were small (4 and 6), so the resulting confidence interval around the mean difference was very wide, almost 40 points on the 0-100 point scale, but you can be 95% confident that if you were to run the studies again, it is unlikely that the observed mean difference would be less than 2.19 or greater than 41.71.

 **TIP:**

> A key advantage of computing a confidence interval around the mean difference is that it helps practitioners address practical as well as statistical significance. In this example, if all you care about is obtaining a statistically significant result, then it doesn't matter whether that difference was 2.19 or 41.71. On the other hand, if you need to be able to claim that the difference is something larger than 2.19, then you're not yet finished with your work. You might need to collect additional data to increase the degrees of freedom and reduce the standard error to increase the precision of measurement. If everything else stays the same (e.g., mean difference and standard deviations), collecting more data will reduce the size of the associated 95% confidence interval.

Comparison of Two Independent Sets of Data: Example 2

For another comparison of independent sets of data, consider a second iteration of the VUI study described previously as the second benchmarking example. That study was conducted using the Wizard of Oz methodology, with a human simulating the system's speech recognition and then playing back planned responses in a synthetic voice. In a follow-up study conducted once the demo was operational, four participants completed the same set of tasks and, at the end of the study, completed the PSSUQ. We thought there was a possibility that once participants were dealing with a real system that their experience might not be as good as when there was a human in the loop. Table 4.7 shows the results.

Participant	SysUse	InfoQual	IntQual	PSSUQ	PSSUQ100
1	2.3	3.0	2.2	2.5	75.0
2	2.4	2.4	3.0	2.6	73.3
3	1.5	1.6	3.0	1.7	88.3
4	1.9	2.9	1.7	2.1	81.7
Mean	2.03	2.48	2.48	2.23	79.58
Std Dev	0.41	0.64	0.64	0.41	6.85
n	4	4	4	4	4
Std Error	0.21	0.32	0.32	0.21	3.43
df	3	3	3	3	3
t(90)	2.35	2.35	2.35	2.35	2.35
d(90)	0.48	0.75	0.75	0.48	8.07
90% Upper	4.38	4.83	4.83	4.58	81.94
90% Lower	1.54	1.72	1.72	1.74	71.52

t-test	
Mean	79.58
Benchmark	71.1
Difference	8.48
Std Error	3.43
t	2.475
df	3
p	0.045

TABLE 4.7: PSSUQ ratings from voice interaction prototype (circa 2000).

Note that these data, like the first set, had a mean (79.58) significantly higher than the benchmark of 71.1 (t(3) = 2.475, p = 0.045). With small sample sizes and a small mean difference, it seems unlikely that the evidence would support rejecting the null hypothesis, but let's run through the steps.

- Subtract one mean from the other to get the mean difference, typically subtracting the smaller mean from the larger (82.38 - 79.58 = 2.80).

- Start getting the standard error by first computing, for each group, the ratio of the square of the standard deviation by the sample size (Iteration 1: $14.36^2/7 = 29.47$, Iteration 2: $6.85^2/4 = 11.75$).

- Finish computing the standard error by adding those ratios together and taking their square root (=SQRT(29.47+11.75) = 6.42).

- Finally, compute t by dividing the mean difference by the standard error (2.80/6.42 = 0.44).

With t and df (and a two-tailed test), the Excel =TDIST function (=TDIST(0.44,9,2) = 0.67. So the conclusion from the formal test is that the difference was not statistically significant (t(9) = 0.44, p = 0.67). It's still possible that with larger samples sizes you might reach a different conclusion, but with the data in hand, the result was inconclusive. To get a more comprehensive idea about this test outcome, let's compute the confidence interval around the mean difference.

- The critical value of t was 2.26 (=TINV(0.05,9))

- Determine the critical difference by multiplying the critical value of t and the standard error (2.26 * 6.42) = 14.5.

- Compute the lower limit of the 95% confidence interval by subtracting the critical difference from the mean difference (2.8 - 14.5 = -11.7).

- Compute the upper limit of the 95% confidence interval by adding the critical difference to the mean difference (2.8 + 14.5 = 17.3).

The 95% confidence interval around the mean difference of 2.8 ranged from -11.7 to 17.3. Because this interval contains 0, the null hypothesis of no difference is plausible, so it can't be rejected. It's important not to make too much of these kinds of results, but the data were consistent with the hypothesis that the Wizard of Oz simulation of the system led to a user experience that was similar to the experience of using the working prototype. The data also showed that we, as a voice user interface design group in the year 2000, had a long way to go to start designing voice-based interactions that could lead to substantially above-average user experiences (a goal we have been pursuing with increasing success for about 20 years).

Comparison of Two Dependent Sets of Data: Example 1

Now widely regarded as the first smartphone, the IBM Simon Personal Communicator (see Figure 4.4) made its first public appearance at Comdex in 1992 using its codename of Angler. Although for various reasons (e.g., expensive, costing over $1000 in 1994 dollars, and having only an hour of talk time) it was not a commercial success, it received acclaim for its interaction design (Lewis, 1996), including Best of Show at Comdex '93.

Because the goal of the Simon was to provide cellular telephony and personal organizer functions (such as address book and calendar), we selected two popular personal organizers to use to establish performance and attitudinal benchmarks for over 30 microtasks (such as add a name to the address book and edit a calendar entry) – the Sharp Wizard 9600 and the HP-95LX. After finishing all the tasks with each product (counterbalancing the order of presentation of products across participants), the four participants completed the PSSUQ to rate their experience. Table 4.8 shows the resulting PSSUQ100 results.

When each participant provides data for each of two products, the analytical focus is on the difference scores. Table 4.8 shows the 95% confidence interval around the difference scores ranging from -32 to 73 (an interval that includes 0), and the formal test also indicated a nonsignificant outcome (t(3) = 1.23, p = 0.30).

FIGURE 4.4: Simon Personal Communicator (pre-production clear-case model) by an iPhone 5.

Participant	Wizard	HP 95LX	Diff
1	61.67	61.67	0.00
2	76.67	23.33	53.33
3	56.67	71.67	-15.00
4	85.00	41.67	43.33
Mean	70.00	49.58	20.42
Std Dev	13.12	21.49	33.06
n	4	4	4
Std Err	6.56	10.74	16.53
df	3	3	3
t(95)	3.18	3.18	3.18
d(95)	20.88	34.19	52.61
Upper limit	90.88	83.78	73.03
Lower limit	49.12	15.39	-32.20
t			1.23
df			3
p			0.30

TABLE 4.8: Comparison of Wizard and 95-LX PSSUQ100 ratings.

Here are the steps for computing the confidence interval around the difference scores (Diff in Table 4.8).

- For each participant, subtract the data for the second product from the first. (I usually set this up so the mean difference will be positive – sometimes Excel has trouble dealing with negative values of t.)

- Take the mean of the column of difference scores (20.42).

- Compute the df by subtracting 1 from the sample size (4 - 1 = 3).

- Use =TINV to get the critical value of t for a 95% confidence interval (=TINV(.05,3) = 3.18).

- Multiply the standard error and the critical value of t to get the critical value of d (16.53 * 3.18 = 52.61).

- Add the critical value of d to the mean difference to get the upper limit (20.42 + 52.61 = 73.03).

- Subtract the critical value of d from the mean difference to get the lower limit (20.42 - 52.61 = -32.20).

And here are the additional steps for computing the formal test of significance.

- Compute the observed value of t by dividing the mean difference by its standard error (20.42/16.53 = 1.23).

- Compute p for this value of t, df, and a two-tailed test (=TDIST(1.23,3,2) = 0.30).

We could have invested in more data collection at this point, but instead we decided that because there was no obvious trend toward one of these products being markedly superior to the other in overall perceived user experience as measured with the PSSUQ, we would establish benchmarks on a task-by-task and measure-by-measure basis, setting the benchmark to whichever product had the best outcome for a given task and measure.

Comparison of Two Dependent Sets of Data: Example 2

After decades of research, low-cost (relatively) speech recognition products featuring continuous speech recognition burst on the scene in the late 1990s, with fierce competition among companies like IBM, Dragon, Philips, and Lernout & Hauspie (Lewis, 2001). As part of IBM's speech product development effort, we routinely conducted usability and accuracy studies of the many different versions of IBM ViaVoice (Figure 4.5) and its competitors.

Table 4.9 shows the overall PSSUQ100 results for an experiment in which eight participants used two different commercially available speech recognition dictation systems (one IBM ViaVoice, the other competitive) to complete a variety of reading transcription tasks (Lewis, 1999). Participants received training in two different correction strategies for both systems: multimodal correction (voice plus mouse plus keyboard) and hands-free correction (voice only), and used both correction strategies with both products during the experiment. The order in which participants worked with the various products and strategies was completely counterbalanced. After participants finished the tasks with both correction strategies with a product, they completed the PSSUQ. As shown in Table 4.9, the 95% confidence interval around the mean difference ranged from 0.33 to 17.17 (excluding 0), and the formal test of the mean difference was statistically significant (t(7) = 2.46, p = 0.04) in favor of IBM ViaVoice.

FIGURE 4.5: IBM ViaVoice continuous speech dictation product.

Participant	IBM	Competitor	Diff
1	100.00	93.33	6.67
2	93.33	100.00	-6.67
3	78.33	68.33	10.00
4	68.33	53.33	15.00
5	76.67	65.00	11.67
6	76.67	51.67	25.00
7	78.33	66.67	11.67
8	41.67	45.00	-3.33
Mean	76.67	67.92	8.75
Std Dev	17.41	19.59	10.07
n	8	8	8
Std Err	6.16	6.93	3.56
df	7	7	7
t(95)	2.36	2.36	2.36
d(95)	14.56	16.38	8.42
Upper limit	91.22	84.30	17.17
Lower limit	62.11	51.54	0.33
t			2.46
df			7
p			0.04

TABLE 4.9: Comparison of PSSUQ100 ratings for two continuous speech dictation products.

CHAPTER SUMMARY & TAKEAWAYS

- One of the most useful PSSUQ/CSUQ analyses is also one of the most basic -- estimating the mean of a set of data, computing a confidence interval around the mean, and interpreting the values with the Sauro-Lewis curved grading scale.

- The most basic comparison is the mean of a set of observations with a benchmark value.

- Once you go beyond simple estimation, you need to be reasonably familiar with formal statistical testing, including what it means to reject or fail to reject the null hypothesis.

- For comparison with benchmarks, use one-tailed testing; for all other analyses, use two-tailed.

- There are two ways to set PSSUQ/CSUQ benchmarks -- ideally with competitive evaluation, but when that isn't available, select a benchmark using the Sauro-Lewis curved grading scale.

- When comparing two sets of data, the appropriate method is different for independent (between-subjects) and dependent (within-subjects) data.

- When appropriate, prefer within-subjects (dependent) experimental designs over between-subjects (independent), but don't forget to counterbalance the order of presentation of the experimental conditions.

## CHAPTER 5

USING THE PSSUQ AND CSUQ: ADVANCED ANALYSES

In Chapter 4, the analyses involved only one set of data (estimation and comparison with a benchmark) or two (independent or dependent) sets of data. Things quickly get more complicated as we increase the number of data sets in an analysis. The primary analytical method for these more complex analyses is the analysis of variance (ANOVA) (Sauro & Lewis, 2016). ANOVA was developed about 100 years ago as a method for the systematic analysis of agricultural data, but was rapidly adopted by other disciplines. It can take years of graduate training to become proficient in ANOVA. In the first section of the chapter we'll cover two topics: multiple comparisons and analysis of interactions (including profile analysis). The second section will cover multiple regression.

TIP:

> When I have access to it, I prefer SPSS for advanced analyses such as ANOVA. Unfortunately, SPSS is an expensive product, with the basic subscription starting at about $100/month at the time of writing this book. When I don't have access to SPSS, I use R. R is a free open source software environment for statistical computing and graphics, available at http://www.r-project.org/. Find the Getting Started panel, then click "download R" – this takes you to a list of CRAN mirrors (CRAN is an acronym for Comprehensive R Archive Network). Each "mirror" is a website from which you can get R. Go down the list to find your country (e.g., USA) and select one of the sites (e.g., http://cran.case.edu/). Depending on the type of computer you have, select the appropriate version of R to download (Linux, Mac OS, or Windows). Select "base." This takes you to the download page for first-time installers. Click the "Download R" link, which downloads an executable (.exe) file that you can double-click to complete the installation (following the on-screen instructions). After installation, there will be an R icon you can use to start the R console.

COMPARISON OF MULTIPLE INDEPENDENT SETS OF DATA

A finding across numerous studies is that users who have more experience with their systems tend to provide higher ratings than those with less experience. That was the case in the study I conducted to replicate the original CSUQ survey (Lewis, 2018b – see Chapter 3 for details). That study had a sample size of 618, making it unrealistic to show individual cases in a table in this book. For the purpose of illustrating the analysis of multiple independent sets of data, Table 5.1 shows a subset of that data, from the first eight respondents for each of three levels of experience (having used the system they were rating for 1 to 10 years, 11 to 20 years, or more than 20 years). Figure 5.1 shows means and 95% confidence intervals for the results.

Notice in the figure how the width of the confidence intervals decrease as the mean rating increases. This often happens because there is more opportunity for variation around a mean close to the center of a scale than one close to the endpoints. For example, if the mean for the most experienced group have been 100, then variability would be 0 because all scores contributing to the mean would have to be 100. Also, there is considerable overlap in the confidence intervals, but as mentioned previously, it is still possible that a statistical test might be significant despite the overlap.

Respondent	Experience	SysUse	InfoQual	IntQual	CSUQ	CSUQ100
1	1to10	4.33	4.83	5.00	4.63	39.6
2	1to10	2.50	3.17	2.00	2.63	72.9
3	1to10	5.50	3.50	4.67	4.50	41.7
4	1to10	3.50	4.83	2.67	3.81	53.1
5	1to10	6.00	6.50	6.00	6.19	13.5
6	1to10	3.83	3.25	3.67	3.86	52.4
7	1to10	1.00	5.00	1.00	2.50	75.0
8	1to10	1.00	1.00	1.00	1.00	100.0
9	11to20	1.50	2.33	1.33	1.75	87.5
10	11to20	1.33	2.00	1.00	1.56	90.6
11	11to20	4.17	5.67	4.00	4.69	38.5
12	11to20	2.00	3.17	1.67	2.38	77.1
13	11to20	2.50	2.67	2.00	2.50	75.0

(continued on pg. 110)

Respon-dent	Experi-ence	SysUse	InfoQual	IntQual	CSUQ	CSUQ100
14	11to20	1.17	2.00	1.00	1.44	92.7
15	11to20	1.80	3.50	2.00	2.53	74.4
16	11to20	3.33	5.00	2.33	3.67	55.6
17	Over20	1.83	2.00	2.00	1.94	84.4
18	Over20	1.17	3.50	2.00	2.25	79.2
19	Over20	1.67	3.50	2.67	2.56	74.0
20	Over20	1.17	2.50	1.00	1.63	89.6
21	Over20	1.00	1.00	1.00	1.00	100.0
22	Over20	1.67	2.50	1.67	2.00	83.3
23	Over20	2.33	3.33	3.00	2.88	68.8
24	Over20	1.67	1.83	1.00	1.63	89.6

TABLE 5.1: Comparison of CSUQ100 ratings for three levels of experience.

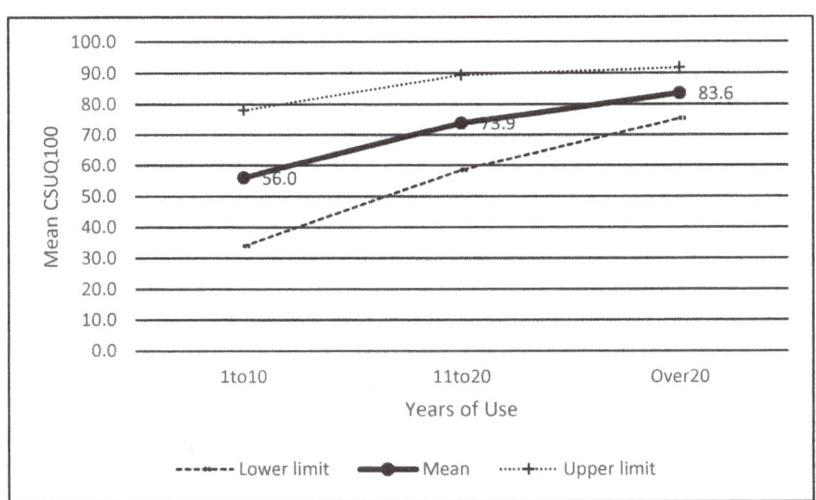

FIGURE 5.1: Means and 95% confidence intervals for CSUQ100 ratings of three levels of experience.

The most common way to analyze this type of finding is to start with what is known as an omnibus one-way ANOVA (one-way because there is just one independent variable with multiple levels). Should that high-level test turn out to be significant, the next step would be to conduct a post-hoc multiple comparisons test to gain insight into which means are significantly different from which other means. That's the strategy I'll illustrate for this book, although some analysts argue that there is no compelling need for the first omnibus ANOVA if you have decided in advance to conduct multiple comparisons (Sauro & Lewis, 2016).

Using SPSS

Figure 5.2 shows the choices made to set up the analysis in SPSS, with the results provided in Table 5.2. To follow the steps in Figure 5.2, after starting SPSS and importing or copying the data from Table 5.1, select Analyze, then General Linear Model, then Univariate. As shown in the Univariate control panel, the Dependent Variable is CSUQ100 and there is one Fixed Factor of Experience. The next panel (displayed after pressing the "Post Hoc …" button) shows the selection of Bonferroni from a large group of post-hoc multiple comparisons methods.

It is beyond the scope of this book to get into detailed differences among the various multiple comparisons methods. In Sauro and Lewis (2016), Jeff Sauro and I provided guidance on our preferred methods. All of these methods provide different levels of control over the increase in the Type I error that occurs when making more than one comparison, just like repeated flipping a coin increases the probably of getting at least one head (even if the coin is biased such that the likelihood of getting a head is just 0.05). Without getting into all the details, two of our preferred methods are Bonferroni and Benjamini-Hochberg. Unfortunately, SPSS does not offer a Benjamini-Hochberg option, but as I'll show below, it isn't difficult to set up by hand.

There's a lot in the SPSS output in Table 5.2, but we only need to focus on a few elements. First, was the omnibus test statistically significant? To determine that, look at the observed significance level ("Sig.") of Experience in the tests of between-subjects effects, which is less than 0.05, indicating statistical significance. The proper way to report that result includes the value of F (which is the ratio of the mean square of Experience divided by the Error mean square), the effect and error degrees of freedom, and the value of p – for this example, "The main effect of Experience was statistically significant ($F(2, 21) = 4.1$, $p = 0.03$." The Bonferroni multiple comparisons include all possible pairs of comparisons, and indicate that the only significant comparison was the one between the means of the 1to10 and Over20 groups. All other comparisons had significance levels (Sig.) substantially greater than 0.05.

Another way to set up Bonferroni multiple comparisons is to run multiple t-tests, but instead of comparing their observed significance levels to 0.05, you compare them to 0.05 divided by the number of t-tests which, for this example, is 3, so the significance criterion is 0.017 (0.05/3). Table 5.3 shows the results of running all three possible combinations of the three levels of the Experience variable. Consistent with the SPSS Bonferroni output in Table 5.2, the only significant comparison (p < 0.017) is 1to10 vs. Over20 (t(14) = -2.77, p = 0.015). The SPSS path to the control panel for setting up these t-tests is Analyze > Compare Means > Independent Groups t-Test.

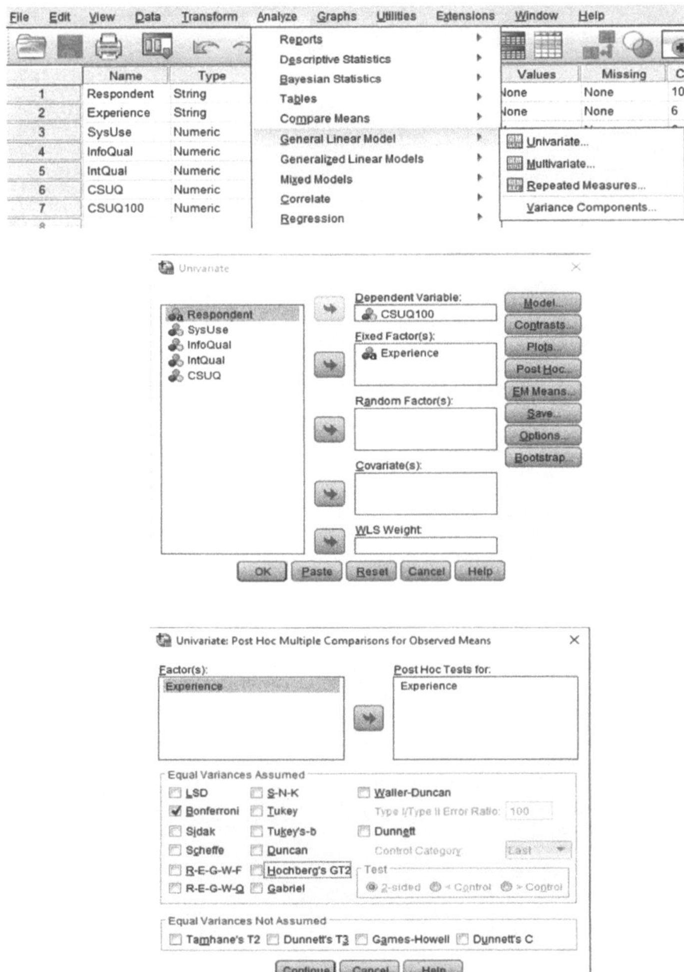

FIGURE 5.2: SPSS setup for ANOVA analysis of CSUQ100 ratings of three levels of experience.

Tests of Between-Subjects Effects					
Dependent Variable: CSUQ100					
Source	Type III Sum of Squares	df	Mean Square	F	Sig.
Corrected Model	3134.207[a]	2	1567.104	4.128	.031
Intercept	121623.844	1	121623.844	320.345	.000
Experience	3134.208	2	1567.104	4.128	.031
Error	7972.959	21	379.665		
Total	132731.010	24			
Corrected Total	11107.166	23			

a. R Squared = .282 (Adjusted R Squared = .214)

Multiple Comparisons						
Dependent Variable: CSUQ100						
Bonferroni						
(I) Experience	(J) Experience	Mean Difference (I-J)	Std. Error	Sig.	95% Confidence Interval	
					Lower Bound	Upper Bound
11to20	1to10	17.90	9.742	.241	-7.44	43.24
	Over20	-9.69	9.742	.994	-35.03	15.66
1to10	11to20	-17.90	9.742	.241	-43.24	7.44
	Over20	-27.59*	9.742	.030	-52.93	-2.24
Over20	11to20	9.69	9.742	.994	-15.66	35.03
	1to10	27.59*	9.742	.030	2.24	52.93

Based on observed means.

The error term is Mean Square(Error) = 379.665.

*. The mean difference is significant at the 0.05 level.

TABLE 5.2: SPSS output for comparison of CSUQ100 ratings for three levels of experience.

Com-parison	Independent Samples Test					95% Confidence	
	t	df	p	Mean Difference	Std Error		
						Lower	Upper
1to10 vs. 11to20	-1.56771	14	0.139269	-17.9	11.41796	-42.3891	6.58909
11to20 vs. Over20	-1.3043	14	0.213168	-9.6875	7.427367	-25.6176	6.242618
1to10 vs. Over20	-2.76967	14	0.015052	-27.5875	9.960568	-48.9508	-6.22421

TABLE 5.3: SPSS output for t-tests for each pairwise combination of Experience levels.

The Benjamini-Hochberg method is similar to Bonferroni, but instead of having the same criterion for all comparisons, there is a sliding scale of criteria from 0.05/N to 0.05, where N is the number of comparisons. With three comparisons, the criteria are 0.017, 0.033, and 0.05. Compare these with the p-values from the multiple t-tests arranged from smallest to largest, which for the tests in Table 5.3 are 0.015, 0.139, and 0.213. For this example, the Benjamini-Hochberg method also indicates just one statistically significant difference, 1to10 vs. Over20 (0.015 < 0.017) – the other two were not statistically significant (0.139 > 0.033; 0.213 > 0.05). Note that the Bonferroni and Benjamini-Hochberg methods will often, but not always, be in agreement. When they disagree, it will be because the Benjamini-Hochberg method has identified more comparisons as being statistically significant due to its sliding scale of significance criteria.

Using R

To do this analysis in R, start R and enter the following commands in its control panel:

```
x <- c('A', 'A', 'A', 'A', 'A', 'A', 'A', 'A', 'B', 'B', 'B', 'B', 'B', 'B', 'B', 'B', 'C', 'C', 'C', 'C', 'C', 'C', 'C', 'C')

y <- c(39.6, 72.9, 41.7, 53.1, 13.5, 52.4, 75.0, 100.0, 87.5, 90.6, 38.5, 77.1, 75.0, 92.7, 74.4, 55.6, 84.4, 79.2, 74.0, 89.6, 100.0, 83.3, 68.8, 89.6)

x_name <- "cond"

y_name <- "rating"
```

```
voices.df <- data.frame(x,y)

names(voices.df) <- c(x_name,y_name)

aov.out <- aov(rating ~ cond, data=voices.df)

summary(aov.out)
```

The first six commands put the data into an R "data frame" so each
CSUQ100 rating is associated with the rated level of experience -- in this
form, you can use standard R functions for ANOVA (of which there are
several). The fifth command uses a standard R function named aov, which
does one-way ANOVA -- placing the output of the ANOVA into a variable
named aov.out. The last command displays a summary (see Table 5.4) of
the ANOVA with the values for F, p, and degrees of freedom needed to
report the result of the analysis.

	Df	Sum Sq	Mean Sq	F	Pr (>F)
cond	2	3134.00	1567.10	4.128	0.0308
Residuals	21	7973.00	379.70		

TABLE 5.4: R output for ANOVA comparison of CSUQ100 ratings for three levels of
experience.

To compute Bonferroni and Benjamini-Hochberg multiple comparisons in R, you can use the following R script:

```
# Bonferroni and Benjamini-Hochberg adjustment

#

# n is the planned number of comparisons

# alpha is the overall desired level of of significance

# The value for Bonferroni is alpha divided by the number of comparisons

# The values for Benjamini-Hochberg use their rank-based approach

#

compute.mcadjustments <- function(n,alpha) {

bonferroni <- alpha/n

cat("\nRESULTS\n\n")

cat("Bonferroni adjustment for critical value of p:",bonferroni,"\n\n")
```

```
cat("Benjamini-Hochberg adjustments for critical values of p","\n")

iteration <- 1

while (iteration < n+1) {

  bh <- iteration*alpha/n

  rank <- paste("Rank ",iteration,":",sep="")

  cat(rank,bh,"\n")

  iteration <- iteration + 1

}

cat("\n")

}
```

To use this custom function, open R, copy and paste the script into the R control panel, then press Enter. After that, you can invoke the function by entering a command like:

```
compute.mcadjustments(3,.05)
```

where the first argument is the number of comparisons you plan to make and the second argument is the value of alpha for this set of comparisons (conventionally set to 0.05).

For this example, there are three pairwise comparisons: 1to10 vs. 11to20, 11to20 vs. Over20, and 1to10 vs. Over20. Figure 5.3 shows the results of using this function with this command. As shown in the figure, the Bonferroni adjustment in this script uses the method of dividing alpha by the number of tests ($0.05/3 = 0.017$). The Benjamini-Hochberg adjustment is a little more complex, with a different criterion of significance for each comparison (0.017, 0.033, 0.05). Note that the smallest criterion is the same as the Bonferroni criterion (0.017) and the largest criterion is equal to alpha (0.05).

The next step is to conduct a t-test for each paired comparison, then to list the comparisons in ascending order of their p-values. Using the method for independent-groups t-tests presented earlier in this chapter, the results of the multiple t-tests were:

- 1to10 vs. Over20: $t(14) = 2.77$, $p = 0.015$
- 1to10 vs. 11to20: $t(14) = 1.57$, $p = 0.139$
- 11to20 vs. Over20: $t(14) = 1.30$, $p = 0.213$

Using the Bonferroni method, the only significant comparison was the first one because it was the only comparison with p < 0.017 (same conclusion as the SPSS Bonferroni analysis). The Benjamini-Hochberg method arrived at the same conclusion because the lowest p-value was lower than the first criterion of 0.017, but the other two were larger than their corresponding criteria (0.139 > 0.033; 0.213 > 0.05).

```
> # Bonferroni and Benjamini-Hochberg adjustment
> #
> # n is the planned number of comparisons
> # alpha is the overall desired level of of significance
> # The value for Bonferroni is alpha divided by the number of comparisons
> # The values for Benjamini-Hochberg use their rank-based approach
> #
> compute.mcadjustments <- function(n,alpha) {
+ bonferroni <- alpha/n
+ cat("\nRESULTS\n\n")
+ cat("Bonferroni adjustment for critical value of p:",bonferroni,"\n\n")
+ cat("Benjamini-Hochberg adjustments for critical values of p","\n")
+ iteration <- 1
+ while (iteration < n+1) {
+ bh <- iteration*alpha/n
+ rank <- paste("Rank ",iteration,":",sep="")
+ cat(rank,bh,"\n")
+ iteration <- iteration + 1
+ }
+ cat("\n")
+ }
>
> compute.mcadjustments(3,.05)

RESULTS

Bonferroni adjustment for critical value of p: 0.01666667

Benjamini-Hochberg adjustments for critical values of p
Rank 1: 0.01666667
Rank 2: 0.03333333
Rank 3: 0.05
```

FIGURE 5.3: Bonferroni and Benjamini-Hochberg adjustments for three comparisons.

COMPARISON OF MULTIPLE DEPENDENT SETS OF DATA

Table 5.5 shows an expanded set of data from the Simon project (see Table 4.8), with the additional data collected using an early version of Simon (Angler).

Participant	Wizard	HP 95-LX	Angler
1	61.67	61.67	80.00
2	76.67	23.33	71.67
3	56.67	71.67	91.67
4	85.00	41.67	51.67
Mean	70.00	49.58	73.75
Std Dev	13.12335	21.48966	16.85312
n	4	4	4
Std Err	6.561673	10.74483	8.426562
df	3	3	3
t(95)	3.182446	3.182446	3.182446
d(95)	20.88217	34.19485	26.81708
Upper limit	90.88	83.78	100.57
Lower limit	49.12	15.39	46.93

TABLE 5.5: PSSUQ100 ratings from competitive evaluation including early version of Simon.

The underlying statistical models for a one-way ANOVA analyzing *dependent* sets of data (also called repeated measures ANOVA) is more complex than the analysis of independent sets (Cliff, 1987). Fortunately, the Bonferroni and Benjamini-Hochberg methods can be applied to the analysis of within-subjects (dependent, repeated measures) experimental designs (Benjamini & Yekutieli, 2001).

Using SPSS

The path to the control panel for repeated measures ANOVA in SPSS is Analyze > General Linear Model > Repeated Measures. The main effect of Product (Wizard vs. 95LX vs. Angler) was not statistically significant $(F(2, 6) = 1.8, p = 0.24)$. The omnibus F test was not significant, but for this exercise we will perform multiple comparisons. Because three products were evaluated, the Bonferroni criterion is $p < 0.017$ (0.05/3) and the Benjamini-Hochberg criteria are, in order, 0.017, 0.033, and 0.05. Table 5.6 shows the three observed significance levels. The Bonferroni and Benjamini-Hochberg procedures both indicate that none of the paired comparisons were statistically significant.

Comparison	Paired Differences					t	df	Sig. (2-tailed)
	Mean	Std. Deviation	Std. Error Mean	95% CI around Diff				
				Lower	Upper			
HP95LX - Angler	-24.16750	16.69803	8.34901	-50.73779	2.40279	-2.895	3	0.063
Wizard - HP95LX	20.41750	33.06633	16.53317	-32.19842	73.03342	1.235	3	0.305
Wizard - Angler	-3.75000	29.66832	14.83416	-50.95892	43.45892	-0.253	3	0.817

TABLE 5.6: Multiple t-tests of early Simon data.

Using R

The first step in using R is to set up the data. R has options for importing larger data sets, but for this example we'll start by defining a series of arrays that match the data in Table 5.5:

```
Participant <- c(1, 2, 3, 4)

Product <- c('Wizard', 'HP95LX', 'Angler')

Wizard <- c(61.67, 76.67, 56.67, 85.00)

HP95LX <- c(61.67, 23.33, 71.67, 41.67)

Angler <- c(80.00, 71.67, 91.67, 51.67)
```

There are a LOT of ways to analyze this type of data using different R packages. To get the same results as SPSS, one way is to install and use the "car" package, which you can get from the R main menu following the path Packages > Install package(s)… and then selecting a source server (CRAN in R terminology) and from that source server, selecting "car." Once you have that package, you can execute the following commands (following a pattern available at Colleen Moore's course for Psychology 610 at http://psych.wisc.edu/moore/Rpdf/610-R8_OneWayWithin.pdf):

```
library(car)

multmodel = lm(cbind(Wizard, HP95LX, Angler) ~ 1)

Trials = factor(c("Wizard", "HP95LX", "Angler"),ordered=F)

model1=Anova(multmodel,idata=data.frame(Trials),idesign=~Trials,type="III")

summary(model1,multivariate=F)
```

In the R script above, the first line opens the "car" library. The second line defines the desired linear model (e.g., binds the ratings from the three products together to show that they are different levels of the repeated-measures independent variable and saves that model in "multmodel"). The third line defines the variable "Trials" as being the name of the factor associated with the different product levels. The fourth line performs the ANOVA using the "car" Anova function, which has three required arguments: the model, the data frame, and the design. It also has a fourth, optional argument that specifies the use of Type III sums of squares in the analysis (the topic of Type I, II, and III sums of squares is beyond the scope of this book, but because the default in SPSS is Type III, that's what was used in this example). The fifth line produces the output of the analysis, shown in Figure 5.4.

```
> Participant <- c(1, 2, 3, 4)
> Product <- c('Wizard', 'HP95LX', 'Angler')
> Wizard <- c(61.67, 76.67, 56.67, 85.00)
> HP95LX <- c(61.67, 23.33, 71.67, 41.67)
> Angler <- c(80.00, 71.67, 91.67, 51.67)
> library(car)
Loading required package: carData
> multmodel = lm(cbind(Wizard, HP95LX, Angler) ~ 1)
> Trials = factor(c("Wizard", "HP95LX", "Angler"),ordered=F)
> model1=Anova(multmodel,idata=data.frame(Trials),idesign=~Trials,type="III")
> summary(model1,multivariate=F)


Univariate Type III Repeated-Measures ANOVA Assuming Sphericity

            Sum Sq num Df Error SS den Df  F value     Pr(>F)
(Intercept)  49840      1   501.96      3 297.8756 0.0004238 ***
Trials        1353      2  2252.42      6   1.8025 0.2437568
---
Signif. codes:  0 '***' 0.001 '**' 0.01 '*' 0.05 '.' 0.1 ' ' 1


Mauchly Tests for Sphericity

       Test statistic p-value
Trials        0.57795 0.57795


Greenhouse-Geisser and Huynh-Feldt Corrections
 for Departure from Sphericity

       GG eps Pr(>F[GG])
Trials 0.70321     0.2609


        HF eps Pr(>F[HF])
Trials 1.137588  0.2437568
Warning message:
In summary.Anova.mlm(model1, multivariate = F) : HF eps > 1 treated as 1
```

FIGURE 5.4: ANOVA results for early Simon competitive PSSUQ100 data.

The key part of this output for our purposes is the result of the F test, which matches the SPSS output (F(2, 6) = 1.8, p = 0.24), indicating no significant difference in the PSSUQ100 ratings of these products. Computing the Bonferroni and Benjamini-Hochberg criteria for R are identical to the steps described above for SPSS. To get the p-values for the multiple t-tests using R, enter:

```
t.test(Angler, HP95LX, paired = TRUE, alternative = "two.sided")

t.test(Wizard, HP95LX, paired = TRUE, alternative = "two.sided")

t.test(Angler, Wizard, paired = TRUE, alternative = "two.sided")
```

The results and conclusions are the same as those obtained with SPSS:

- Angler vs. HP05LX: t(3) = 2.895, p = 0.063
- Wizard vs. HP95LX: t(3) = 1.235, p = 0.305
- Angler vs. Wizard: t(3) = 0.253, p = 0.817

ANALYZING INTERACTION WITH INDEPENDENT SETS OF DATA

One of the applications of ANOVA is the assessment of factorial designs (the manipulation of multiple independent variables in the same study). With ANOVA, you can evaluate the significance of main effects (the effects of each of the independent variables) and their interaction (the extent to which the effects of one variable are dependent on the levels of the other variables in the experiment). The simplest factorial design is one in which there are two independent variables, each with two levels (known as a 2 × 2 factorial design). With regard to underlying statistical models, the simplest 2 x 2 factorial design has no repeated measures.

To demonstrate the analysis of a 2 x 2 factorial design, we return to the previously used ratings from usability studies of a voice interaction demo and prototype (see Tables 4.6 and 4.7). New to this table is information about the gender of each participant. With this information, it is possible to assess the statistical significance of the main effects of study (Demo or Prototype) and Gender (Female or Male) and their interaction.

Participant	Study	Gender	SysUse	InfoQual	IntQual	PSSUQ	PSSUQ100
1	Demo	F	1.5	1.4	1.0	1.3	95.0
2	Demo	M	2.0	2.0	2.0	2.0	83.3
3	Demo	F	4.0	2.9	2.7	3.4	60.0
4	Demo	M	1.6	1.0	1.3	1.3	95.0
5	Demo	F	1.8	3.4	1.7	2.3	78.3
6	Demo	M	1.0	1.3	1.7	1.2	96.7
7	Demo	M	2.8	3.0	3.0	2.9	68.3
8	Prototype	M	2.3	3.0	2.2	2.5	75.0
9	Prototype	M	2.4	2.4	3.0	2.6	73.3
10	Prototype	F	1.5	1.6	3.0	1.7	88.3
11	Prototype	F	1.9	2.9	1.7	2.1	81.7

TABLE 5.7: PSSUQ ratings and participant genders from voice interaction prototype (circa 2000).

Figure 5.5 shows the graph of the interaction between study and gender. Interactions can take various forms, from parallel to crossed lines. The lines are crossed in Figure 5.5, suggesting that the user experience in the different studies might not have been the same for males and females. The F-test of the interaction will reveal whether the observed data, suggesting an interaction, were significantly different from the parallel lines you expect when there is no interaction. In other words, the null hypothesis (Ho) is that there is no interaction, and the test of significance will tell us how likely we are to get these data if the null hypothesis of no interaction is true.

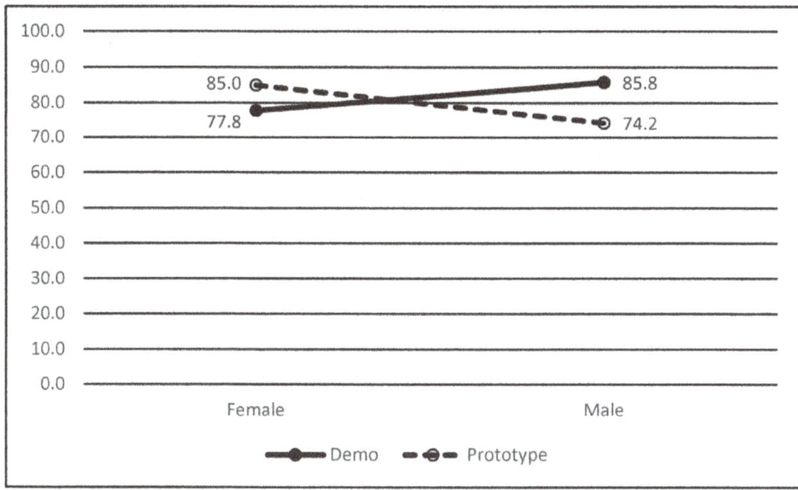

FIGURE 5.5: Interaction between study and gender.

TIP:

Significant crossed interactions discovered when conducting user research should be of particular interest to UX designers because they suggest a need for more complexity in the design to support the different needs of different user groups (e.g., additional settings). Fortunately, crossed interactions in the human-computer interaction literature are relatively rare; it's more common to find significant interactions involving two user groups where a difference in design helps one user group without having a negative effect on the other (Lewis, 2012).

Using SPSS

After importing or copying the data from Table 5.7 into SPSS, the path to the control panel to set up the two-way ANOVA is: Analyze > General linear model > Univariate. Figure 5.6 shows the control panel setup, and Table 5.8 shows the results. The key findings were:

- No significant main effect of Study ($F(1, 7) = 0.76$, $p = 0.791$)
- No significant main effect of Gender ($F(1, 7) = 0.03$, $p = 0.868$)
- No significant Study by Gender interaction ($F(1, 7) = 1.372$, $p = 0.280$)

These nonsignificant results are not surprising given the amount of variability in the data and the small sample size.

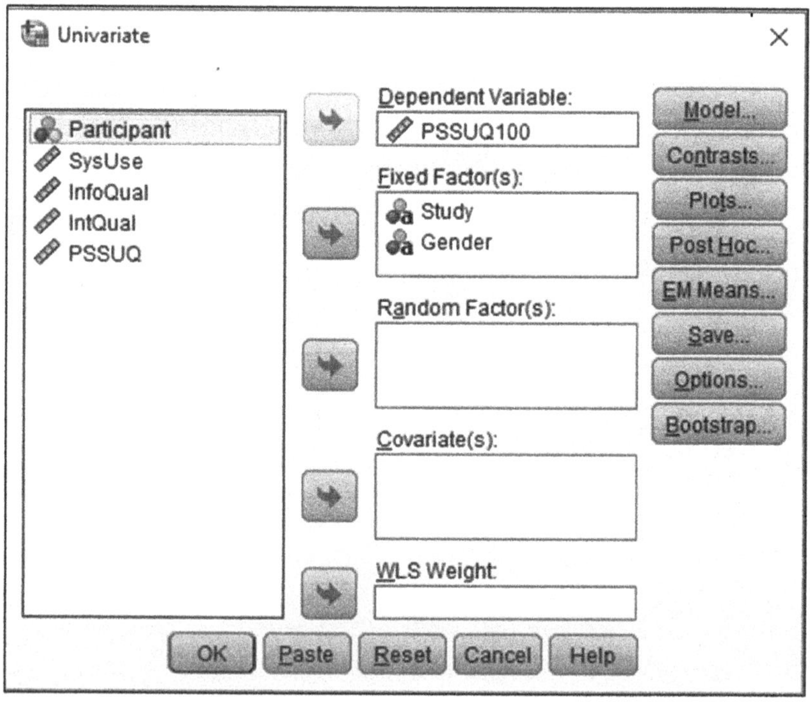

FIGURE 5.6: Setting up the 2 × 2 analysis in SPSS.

Tests of Between-Subjects Effects					
Dependent Variable: PSSUQ100					
Source	Type III Sum of Squares	df	Mean Square	F	Sig.
Corrected Model	248.948[a]	3	82.983	.504	.691
Intercept	65786.642	1	65786.642	399.711	.000
Study	12.460	1	12.460	.076	.791
Gender	4.922	1	4.922	.030	.868
Study * Gender	225.805	1	225.805	1.372	.280
Error	1152.099	7	164.586		
Total	74205.230	11			
Corrected Total	1401.047	10			

a. R Squared = .178 (Adjusted R Squared = -.175)

TABLE 5.8: Results of SPSS 2 x 2 ANOVA.

Using R

To set up this 2 x 2 analysis in R, use the following commands:

```
p <- c(1,2,3,4,5,6,7,8,9,10,11)

s <- c('Demo','Demo','Demo','Demo','Demo','Demo','Demo','Prototype',
    'Prototype','Prototype','Prototype')

g <- c('F','M','F','M','F','M','M','M','M','F','F')

y <- c(95.0,83.3,60.0,95.0,78.3,96.7,68.3,75.0,73.3,88.3,81.7)


p_name <- "product"

s_name <- "study"

g_name <- "gender"

y_name <- "rating"


voices.df <- data.frame(p, s, g, y)

names(voices.df) <- c(p_name,s_name,g_name,y_name)


options(contrasts = c("contr.helmert", "contr.poly"))
```

```
voices.df$study <- as.factor(voices.df$study)

voices.df$gender <- as.factor(voices.df$gender)

library(car)

my_anova <- lm(rating~study*gender,data=voices.df)

Anova(my_anova, type = "III")
```

The results of the analysis are in Figure 5.7.

```
Anova Table (Type III tests)

Response: rating
              Sum Sq Df  F value    Pr(>F)
(Intercept)    65787  1 399.7108 1.96e-07 ***
study             12  1   0.0757   0.7911
gender             5  1   0.0299   0.8676
study:gender     226  1   1.3720   0.2798
Residuals       1152  7
---
Signif. codes:  0 '***' 0.001 '**' 0.01 '*' 0.05 '.' 0.1 ' ' 1
```

FIGURE 5.7: Results of 2 × 2 analysis in R.

TIP:

Due to differences in analytical defaults, results of ANOVA in R do not necessarily match SPSS results unless the R defaults are modified to produce results consistent with SPSS (neither set of defaults are wrong or right – they are just different). The key parts of the R script above that change those defaults are the contrasts in the "options" command and the specification of Type III sums-of-squares in the "Anova" command, so if it important to obtain results consistent with SPSS, be sure to include them in the analysis (for more details and another example, see http://www.statscanbefun.com/rblog/2015/8/27/ensuring-r-generates-the-same-anova-f-values-as-spss).

A SPECIAL TYPE OF INTERACTION: PROFILE ANALYSIS

Standardized usability questionnaires like the PSSUQ/CSUQ that have more than one contributing factor have a disadvantage relative to unidimensional measures because they typically require more items to assess their multiple factors. Their corresponding advantage is the additional information provided by the subscales defined by the factor structure.

One way to explore how different aspects of design or different user groups affect PSSUQ/CSUQ subscales is to conduct a profile analysis. A profile analysis is an ANOVA in which one of the independent variables is a repeated-measures variable made up of a questionnaire's subscales. For the PSSUQ/CSUQ, that would be SysUse, InfoQual, and IntQual.

To illustrate how to conduct a profile analysis, we'll return to the data in Table 5.1, this time converting the subscale data to a 0-100-point scale for easier interpretation (see Table 5.9), keeping in mind that the subscale means are NOT interpretable using the Sauro-Lewis curved grading scale (see Chapter 3, Lewis, 2018b). Figure 5.8 shows the interaction between level of experience and the CSUQ100 subscales. The lines in the profile seem to be close to parallel (no interaction), with the exception of similar IntQual100 ratings for 11to20 and Over20, keeping open the possibility of significant interaction.

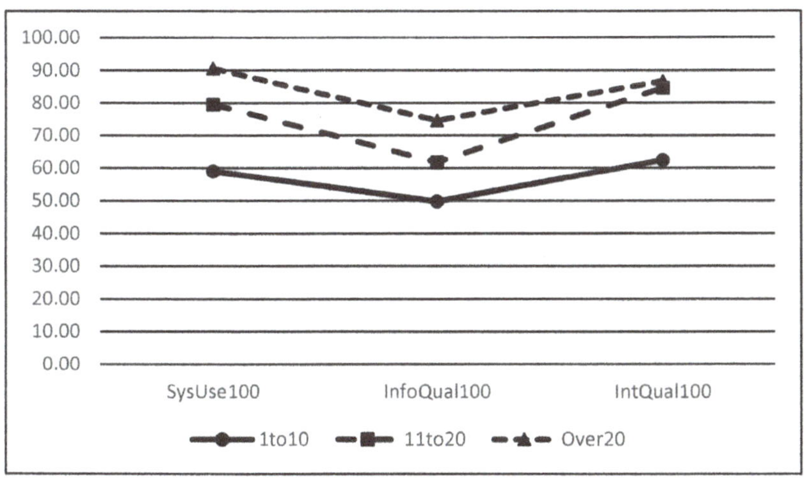

FIGURE 5.8: Interaction of three levels of experience with CSUQ100 subscales.

Respon-dent	Used	SysUse100	InfoQual100	IntQual100	CSUQ100
1	1to10	44.50	36.11	33.33	39.6
2	1to10	75.00	63.89	83.33	72.9
3	1to10	25.00	58.33	38.89	41.7
4	1to10	58.33	36.11	72.22	53.1
5	1to10	16.67	8.33	16.67	13.5
6	1to10	52.78	62.50	55.56	52.4
7	1to10	100.00	33.33	100.00	75.0
8	1to10	100.00	100.00	100.00	100.0
9	11to20	91.67	77.78	94.44	87.5
10	11to20	94.44	83.33	100.00	90.6
11	11to20	47.22	22.22	50.00	38.5
12	11to20	83.33	63.89	88.89	77.1
13	11to20	75.00	72.22	83.33	75.0
14	11to20	97.22	83.33	100.00	92.7
15	11to20	86.67	58.33	83.33	74.4
16	11to20	61.11	33.33	77.78	55.6
17	Over20	86.11	83.33	83.33	84.4
18	Over20	97.22	58.33	83.33	79.2
19	Over20	88.89	58.33	72.22	74.0
20	Over20	97.22	75.00	100.00	89.6
21	Over20	100.00	100.00	100.00	100.0
22	Over20	88.89	75.00	88.89	83.3
23	Over20	77.78	61.11	66.67	68.8
24	Over20	88.89	86.11	100.00	89.6

TABLE 5.9: Comparison of CSUQ100 subscale ratings for three levels of experience.

Using SPSS

After importing or copying the data from Table 5.9 into SPSS, the path to the control panel to set up the profile analysis is: Analyze > General linear model > Repeated Measures. Figure 5.9 shows the control panel setup (two steps – first to define the repeated measures variable, then to define the other variables), and Table 5.10 shows the results. The key findings were:

- Significant main effect of Subscales ($F(2, 42) = 14.7$, $p < 0.0001$)

- Significant main effect of Experience ($F(2, 21) = 3.874$, $p = 0.037$)

- No significant Subscales x Experience interaction ($F(4, 42) = 0.85$, $p = 0.502$)

When conducting this type of analysis with the PSSUQ or CSUQ, there will always be a significant main effect of Subscales because they are measuring different aspects of the user experience, so this is not useful information for UX designers or researchers. Note that the main effect of Experience was significant, just as it was when we analyzed the overall CSUQ100 from this table at the beginning of the chapter. The most important new finding was that there was no significant interaction, so for the three subscales, it appears that their profiles are the same for each level of experience (at least, not proved to be different).

TIP:

The findings above are from Table 5.10 assuming that the data meet the assumption of sphericity. The other choices in the table (Greenhouse-Geisser, Huynh-Feldt, and Lower-bound) are alternative methods that adjust the magnitude of the degrees of freedom in the analysis based on the extent to which the assumption of sphericity is not met, usually assessed with Mauchly's test of sphericity. When all of the methods are in agreement with regard to statistical significance, you don't need to worry about this, but if the different methods give different results, you should either check the Mauchly test or just use one of the more conservative methods (e.g., I like Greenhouse-Geisser).

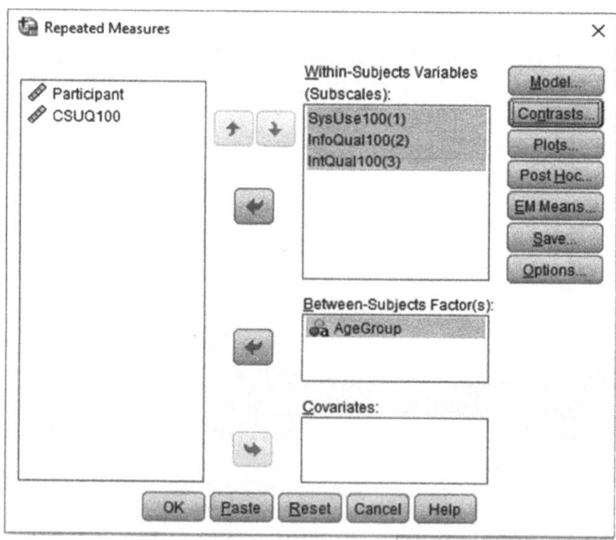

FIGURE 5.9: SPSS setup for profile analysis of CSUQ100 subscale ratings of three levels of experience.

Tests of Within-Subjects Effects

Measure: MEASURE_1

Source		Type III Sum of Squares	df	Mean Square	F	Sig.
Subscales	Sphericity Assumed	3687.436	2	1843.718	14.707	.000
	Greenhouse-Geisser	3687.436	1.278	2886.414	14.707	.000
	Huynh-Feldt	3687.436	1.453	2537.492	14.707	.000
	Lower-bound	3687.436	1.000	3687.436	14.707	.001
Subscales * AgeGroup	Sphericity Assumed	426.312	4	106.578	.850	.502
	Greenhouse-Geisser	426.312	2.555	166.852	.850	.463
	Huynh-Feldt	426.312	2.906	146.682	.850	.474
	Lower-bound	426.312	2.000	213.156	.850	.442
Error(Subscales)	Sphericity Assumed	5265.227	42	125.363		
	Greenhouse-Geisser	5265.227	26.828	196.260		
	Huynh-Feldt	5265.227	30.517	172.535		
	Lower-bound	5265.227	21.000	250.725		

TABLE 5.10: Results of SPSS profile analysis. *(continued on pg. 135)*

Tests of Between-Subjects Effects					
Measure: MEASURE_1					
Transformed Variable: Average					
Source	Type III Sum of Squares	df	Mean Square	F	Sig.
Intercept	375034.292	1	375034.292	320.899	.000
AgeGroup	9055.862	2	4527.931	3.874	.037
Error	24542.647	21	1168.697		

TABLE 5.10: Results of SPSS profile analysis.

Using R

First, we need to open the "car" library, specify the contrasts needed to obtain output consistent with SPSS, and get the data into a data frame.

```
library(car)

options(contrasts = c("contr.helmert", "contr.poly"))

experience <- c('1to10','1to10','1to10','1to10','1to10','1to10','1to10','1to10','11
to20','11to20','11to20','11to20','11to20','11to20','11to20','11to20','Over20','Ov
er20','Over20','Over20','Over20','Over20','Over20','Over20')

sysuse100 <- c(44.50,75.00,25.00,58.33,16.67,52.78,100.00,100.00,91.67,94.44
,47.22,83.33,75.00,97.22,86.67,61.11,86.11,97.22,88.89,97.22,100.00,88.89,77.
78,88.89)

infoqual100 <- c(36.11,63.89,58.33,36.11,8.33,62.50,33.33,100.00,77.78,83.33,
22.22,63.89,72.22,83.33,58.33,33.33,83.33,58.33,58.33,75.00,100.00,75.00,61.1
1,86.11)

intqual100 <- c(33.33,83.33,38.89,72.22,16.67,55.56,100.00,100.00,94.44,100.0
0,50.00,88.89,83.33,100.00,83.33,77.78,83.33,83.33,72.22,100.00,100.00,88.89,
66.67,100.00)

profile.df <- data.frame(experience,sysuse100,infoqual100,intqual100)

profile.df
```

The next lines of the R script specify a variable named "subscale" that includes sysuse100, infoqual100, and intqual100, along with an associated data frame (idata).

```
subscale <- factor(rep(c("sysuse100", "infoqual100", "intqual100"), each=1),
levels=c("sysuse100", "infoqual100", "intqual100"))

idata <- data.frame(subscale)

idata
```

The last three lines define the linear model, conduct the ANOVA, and report the results, which, assuming sphericity, were identical to the SPSS output (see Figure 5.10).

```
mod.ok <- lm(cbind(sysuse100,infoqual100,intqual100) ~ experience,
data=profile.df)

(av.ok <- Anova(mod.ok, idata=idata, idesign=~subscale, type=3))

summary(av.ok, multivariate=FALSE)
```

```
Univariate Type III Repeated-Measures ANOVA Assuming Sphericity

                      Sum Sq num Df Error SS den Df  F value     Pr(>F)
(Intercept)            375034      1  24542.6     21 320.8994 3.354e-14 ***
experience               9056      2  24542.6     21   3.8743   0.03697 *
subscale                 3687      2   5265.2     42  14.7071 1.441e-05 ***
experience:subscale       426      4   5265.2     42   0.8502   0.50161
---
Signif. codes:  0 `***' 0.001 `**' 0.01 `*' 0.05 `.' 0.1 ` ' 1
```

FIGURE 5.10: Results of conducting profile analysis with R.

MULTIPLE REGRESSION

A common research activity is to try to understand the relationships among various metrics. When a questionnaire has psychometrically validated subscales, it may be of interest to assess the extent to which the different subscales affect the values of another measurement. At the end of Chapter 3, Table 3.16 summarized research showing the correspondence between the CSUQ and SUS as measures of perceived usability. The concurrent collection of CSUQ and SUS data allows the assessment of the extent to which the CSUQ subscales are differentially associated with the SUS scores. Table 5.11 shows the first 25 cases from the full set of data collected in Lewis (2018b), used to illustrate this type of multiple regression model. To make it easier to interpret, the CSUQ subscale values in the table have all been converted to 0-100-point scales.

Response	SysUse100	InfoQual100	IntQual100	CSUQ100	SUS
1	91.67	77.78	94.44	87.50	97.50
2	100.00	91.67	88.89	94.79	97.50
3	80.56	75.00	72.22	77.08	80.00
4	44.44	36.11	33.33	39.58	52.50
5	97.22	58.33	83.33	79.17	85.00
6	75.00	63.89	83.33	72.92	87.50
7	25.00	58.33	38.89	41.67	60.00
8	58.33	36.11	72.22	53.13	60.00
9	86.11	83.33	83.33	84.38	50.00
10	77.78	41.67	66.67	61.46	60.00
11	69.44	61.11	66.67	65.63	62.50
12	47.22	22.22	50.00	38.54	30.00
13	69.44	66.67	66.67	68.75	75.00
14	36.67	0.00	83.33	39.39	27.50
15	27.78	19.44	5.56	18.75	45.00
16	83.33	63.89	88.89	77.08	37.50
17	83.33	30.56	61.11	58.33	85.00
18	100.00	55.56	100.00	82.22	100.00
19	16.67	8.33	16.67	13.54	32.50
20	75.00	72.22	83.33	75.00	37.50
21	52.78	62.50	55.56	52.38	82.50
22	0.00	50.00	0.00	18.75	50.00
23	22.22	27.78	83.33	37.50	27.50
24	88.89	58.33	72.22	73.96	72.50
25	83.33	75.00	88.89	81.25	77.50

TABLE 5.11: Concurrently collected CSUQ100 subscale and SUS scores.

TIP:

As with ANOVA, there is a vast array of techniques for regression analysis. In this section I only show one example of multiple linear regression, and focus on just a few associated statistics. If you have a need for more advanced analyses, be sure to consult with a professional statistician.

Using SPSS

After importing or copying the data from Table 5.11 into SPSS, the path to the control panel to set up the regression analysis is: Analyze > Regression > Linear. Figure 5.11 shows the control panel setup and Table 5.12 shows the results.

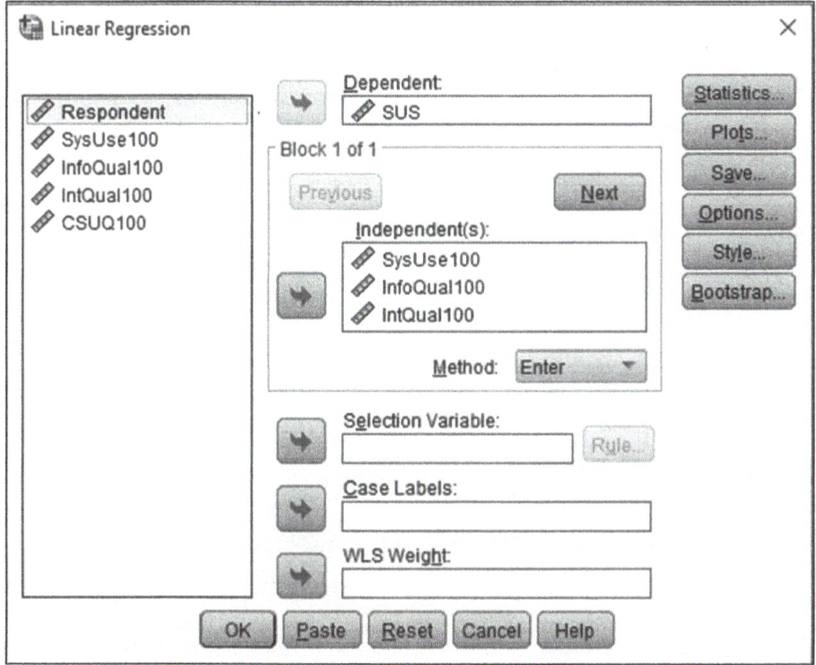

FIGURE 5.11: SPSS setup for multiple regression analysis of relationship between CSUQ100 subscales and SUS scores.

Model Summary				
Model	R	R Square	Adjusted R Square	Std. Error of the Estimate
1	.736[a]	.542	.477	16.87931

a. Predictors: (Constant), IntQual100, InfoQual100, SysUse100

ANOVA[a]						
Model		Sum of Squares	df	Mean Square	F	Sig.
1	Regression	7087.866	3	2362.622	8.292	.001[b]
	Residual	5983.134	21	284.911		
	Total	13071.000	24			

a. Dependent Variable: SUS

b. Predictors: (Constant), IntQual100, InfoQual100, SysUse100

Coefficients[a]						
Model		Unstandardized Coefficients		Standardized Coefficients		
		B	Std. Error	Beta	t	Sig.
1	(Constant)	28.549	9.747		2.929	.008
	SysUse100	.598	.219	.738	2.725	.013
	InfoQual100	.286	.188	.293	1.519	.144
	IntQual100	-.283	.201	-.333	-1.406	.174

a. Dependent Variable: SUS

TABLE 5.12: Results of SPSS multiple regression.

SPSS provides three categories of results: Model Summary, ANOVA, and Coefficients. In the Model Summary, the most important result is the Adjusted R Square which, for these data, is 0.477. A common interpretation of this statistic is that variation in the independent variables of SysUse100, InfoQual100, and IntQual100 accounts for 47.7% of the variation in the dependent variable (SUS). The ANOVA result is a test to see if the overall regression model was statistically significant, which it was it was (F(3, 21) = 8.292, p < 0.001).

The Coefficients results can be used in at least two ways. First, if you wanted a formula that estimated SUS scores from the scores of the three independent variables, that formula would be SUS = 28.549 + 0.598(SysUse100) + 0.286(InfoQual100) – 0.283(IntQual100). If you're more interested in understanding which of the independent variables have the strongest effect on the dependent variable, you can examine the beta (standardized) coefficients. For these data, the only independent variable that was significantly associated with the dependent variable was SysUse100 (t(21) = 2.725, p = 0.013). The effects of the other two independent variables were not statistically significant (InfoQual100: t(21) = 1.519, p = 0.144; IntQual100: t(21) = -1.406, p = 0.174). The degrees of freedom to use for these t-tests is from the Residual row of the ANOVA section of the output. Also, the importance indicated by a beta weight depends only on its magnitude, whether it is positive or negative is irrelevant.

NOTE: These findings were from a subset of a larger data set. This subset is too small to draw meaningful conclusions about nonsignificant outcomes, so please view these results as examples, not as scientifically proven. For example, when I conducted this same analysis on the entire data set (n = 617), all three CSUQ subscales were found to significantly contribute to the modeling of variation in the SUS, with SysUse having the largest contribution (beta = 0.470) and InfoQual and IntQual having smaller and roughly equal contributions (betas of 0.188 and 0.174, respectively).

Using R

To replicate this analysis in R, the first step is to get the data into a data frame.

```
Response <- c(1,2,3,4,5,6,7,8,9,10,11,12,13,14,15,16,17,18,19,20,21,22,23,24,25)

SysUse100 <- c(91.67,100.00,80.56,44.44,97.22,75.00,25.00,58.33,86.11,77.78,69.44,47.22,69.44,36.67,27.78,83.33,83.33,100.00,16.67,75.00,52.78,0.00,22.22,88.89,83.33)

InfoQual100 <- c(77.78,91.67,75.00,36.11,58.33,63.89,58.33,36.11,83.33,41.67,61.11,22.22,66.67,0.00,19.44,63.89,30.56,55.56,8.33,72.22,62.50,50.00,27.78,58.33,75.00)
```

```
IntQual100 <- c(94.44,88.89,72.22,33.33,83.33,83.33,38.89,72.22,83.33,66.67,6
6.67,50.00,66.67,83.33,5.56,88.89,61.11,100.00,16.67,83.33,55.56,0.00,83.33,72
.22,88.89)

CSUQ100 <- c(87.50,94.79,77.08,39.58,79.17,72.92,41.67,53.13,84.38,61.46,6
5.63,38.54,68.75,39.39,18.75,77.08,58.33,82.22,13.54,75.00,52.38,18.75,37.50,7
3.96,81.25)

SUS <- c(97.50,97.50,80.00,52.50,85.00,87.50,60.00,60.00,50.00,60.00,62.50,
30.00,75.00,27.50,45.00,37.50,85.00,100.00,32.50,37.50,82.50,50.00,27.50,72
.50,77.50)

mregdata.df <- data.frame(Response, SysUse100, InfoQual100, IntQual100,
CSUQ100, SUS)
```

The second step is to define the linear model and display the results
(shown in Figure 5.12).

```
mregmodel <- lm(SUS ~ SysUse100 + InfoQual100 + IntQual100,
data=mregdata.df)

summary(mregmodel)
```

```
Coefficients:
            Estimate Std. Error t value Pr(>|t|)
(Intercept)  28.5492     9.7469   2.929  0.00802 **
SysUse100     0.5976     0.2193   2.725  0.01269 *
InfoQual100   0.2862     0.1884   1.519  0.14375
IntQual100   -0.2828     0.2012  -1.406  0.17445
---
Signif. codes:  0 '***' 0.001 '**' 0.01 '*' 0.05 '.' 0.1 ' ' 1

Residual standard error: 16.88 on 21 degrees of freedom
Multiple R-squared:  0.5423,    Adjusted R-squared:  0.4769
F-statistic: 8.292 on 3 and 21 DF,  p-value: 0.0007886
```

FIGURE 5.12: Results of conducting multiple regression with R.

Although the output has different formatting, the results shown match
those obtained with SPSS.

Missing from the R output, however, are the beta weights.
Mathematically, the beta weights are the estimates of the regression coefficients when all the variables (independent and dependent) have been

standardized (i.e., converted into z-scores by subtraction from the mean and division by the standard deviation of the sample data). The following R script shows how to standardize the measures, then runs the multiple regression analysis again, this time with the standardized measures. As shown in Figure 5.13, the estimated coefficients, presented in exponential format (e.g., 7.38e-01 = 0.738), match the beta weights from the SPSS output.

```
SysUse100std <- (SysUse100 - mean(SysUse100))/sd(SysUse100)

InfoQual100std <- (InfoQual100 - mean(InfoQual100))/sd(InfoQual100)

IntQual100std <- (IntQual100 - mean(IntQual100))/sd(IntQual100)

CSUQ100std <- (CSUQ100 - mean(CSUQ100))/sd(CSUQ100)

SUSstd <- (SUS - mean(SUS))/sd(SUS)

mregdatastd.df <- data.frame(Response, SysUse100std, InfoQual100std,
IntQual100std, CSUQ100std, SUSstd)

mregmodelstd <- lm(SUSstd ~ SysUse100std + InfoQual100std +
IntQual100std, data=mregdatastd.df)

summary(mregmodelstd)
```

```
Call:
lm(formula = SUSstd ~ SysUse100std + InfoQual100std + IntQual100std,
    data = mregdatastd.df)

Residuals:
    Min      1Q  Median      3Q     Max
-1.4564 -0.2329  0.0974  0.3471  1.0317

Coefficients:
                 Estimate Std. Error t value Pr(>|t|)
(Intercept)     1.661e-16  1.447e-01   0.000   1.0000
SysUse100std    7.380e-01  2.708e-01   2.725   0.0127 *
InfoQual100std  2.933e-01  1.931e-01   1.519   0.1438
IntQual100std  -3.327e-01  2.367e-01  -1.406   0.1745
---
Signif. codes:  0 '***' 0.001 '**' 0.01 '*' 0.05 '.' 0.1 ' ' 1

Residual standard error: 0.7233 on 21 degrees of freedom
Multiple R-squared:  0.5423,     Adjusted R-squared:  0.4769
F-statistic: 8.292 on 3 and 21 DF,  p-value: 0.0007886
```

FIGURE 5.13: Results of computing beta weights with R.

- For advanced analysis using the PSSUQ/CSUQ, use a professional software package like SPSS or R.

- Common advanced analytical methods include ANOVA, multiple comparisons, and multiple regression.

- One-way ANOVA addresses extensions of the t-test to consider simultaneous comparison of more than two means.

- Two-way ANOVA allows the assessment of interactions, including profile analysis.

- There are many approaches to multiple comparison -- the examples in this chapter include the Bonferroni and Benjamini-Hochberg methods.

- The simplest ANOVA is a one-way analysis of multiple independent sets of data (between-subjects experimental design).

- The statistical model for one-way analysis of multiple dependent sets of data (within-subjects) experimental design is more complex, but the multiple comparison methods are the same.

- Analysis of interactions with ANOVA can lead to insights regarding when it may be necessary for designs to accommodate different types of users.

- Profile analysis is a type of ANOVA that is especially suitable for analyses that include multidimensional measures such as the PSSUQ/CSUQ subscales.

- UX researchers can use multiple regression to understand the relationships among various objective and subjective usability metrics (such as the PSSUQ/CSUQ subscales).

## CHAPTER 6

FUTURE OF THE PSSUQ AND CSUQ

As I finished writing this book in early 2019, the PSSUQ and CSUQ had just passed their 30th anniversary. These questionnaires are two of the most widely-used instruments for standardized assessment of perceived usability and, consequently, user experience. The number of citations of Lewis (1995) tracked by Google Scholar continues to grow month by month, now just over 2000.

Even though it is not the most popular measure of perceived usability, an honor that belongs to the SUS, the PSSUQ and CSUQ are likely to continue being used for the foreseeable future for a number of reasons:

- Once a questionnaire has been selected and used in practice or research, its likelihood of continued use is high when there is value in tracking its measurements over time.

- They occupy a unique place in the taxonomy of UX questionnaires.

- Recent research has indicated that PSSUQ/CSUQ means can be interpreted using the Sauro-Lewis curved grading scale originally developed for the SUS.

Additional areas of research that would expand the usefulness of the PSSUQ/CSUQ for practitioners and researchers are:

- Translation into additional languages

- Replication of correspondence findings with different products and contexts of research

THE PLACE OF THE PSSUQ/CSUQ IN THE TAXONOMY OF UX QUESTIONNAIRES

In Chapter 8 of Quantifying the User Experience (Sauro & Lewis, 2016), Jeff Sauro and I reviewed over 20 published standardized measures of perceived usability and related UX features (e.g., loyalty, trust, technology acceptance). The PSSUQ/CSUQ occupy a unique place in this group of instruments by virtue of the combination of the following characteristics:

- License-free use
- General measure of perceived usability (as opposed to being, for example, Web specific)
- Relatively large number of items but with those items supporting measurement of three subscales
- Overall mean score interpretable using the Sauro-Lewis curved grading scale

When there is a need for an ultra-short measure of perceived usability, the instrument of choice should be the two-item UMUX-LITE (Lewis, 2018b, 2018c, 2018d; Sauro & Lewis, 2016). The 10-item SUS is still an excellent choice, especially given that the Sauro-Lewis curved grading scale was based on hundreds of studies that used the SUS. When there is a need for a multidimensional measure that includes an assessment of information quality (InfoQual), the 16-item PSSUQ/CSUQ fulfills that need. Also, researchers and enterprises that already have an investment in using the PSSUQ/CSUQ have a vested interest in continuing to use it for historical purposes and, as long as the length of the questionnaire is tolerable in their research context, they have no compelling reason to discontinue its use.

USING THE CORRESPONDENCE WITH SUS TO INTERPRET PSSUQ/CSUQ MEANS

The recent research in the correspondence between concurrently collected CSUQ and SUS scores, showing that the means can reasonably be interpreted using the Sauro-Lewis curved grading scale (see the end of Chapter 3), is an extremely important finding. Developing measurement norms is a difficult, time-consuming effort. The discovery of its correspondence with the SUS has allowed the PSSUQ/CSUQ to leapfrog over that effort.

This means that with the relatively simple computational step of converting standard PSSUQ/CSUQ scores to PSSUQ100/CSUQ100 scores, user experience practitioners can use the curved grading scale in Table 3.1 to judge obtained PSSUQ100/CSUQ100 means as indicative of having poor, average, or good levels of perceived usability, presumably driven by having had poor, average, or good user experiences with the rated product/system. It is likely that once this finding has made its way through the UX researcher and practitioner communities, the use of the PSSUQ/CSUQ will increase in the contexts of research and practice for which it is appropriate.

TRANSLATION INTO ADDITIONAL LANGUAGES

For now, the only languages in which the PSSUQ/CSUQ is available are English and Turkish. I hope that UX researchers for whom their primary language is not English or Turkish will take an interest in translating the questionnaire, using the method of Erdinç and Lewis (2013, described in Chapter 3) as a model. In addition to expanding the availability of the PSSUQ/CSUQ to new UX research communities, this would allow more cross-cultural research.

REPLICATION OF CORRESPONDENCE FINDINGS

To date, the assessment of the correspondence between the CSUQ and SUS is based on seven data points (see Table 3.16). This is a reasonable start and the results to date are promising, but the meta-analysis would benefit from the inclusion of correspondence findings from different products and contexts of research. This will only happen if researchers and practitioners routinely collect multiple measurements of perceived usability in which they include, at a minimum, the PSSUQ/CSUQ and the SUS, and then publish those results (or find some other way to share them with the UX research community). This will enable researchers to add rows to Table 3.16 with new data, increasing confidence in the findings. Increased confidence in correspondence is likely to lead to increased use of the PSSUQ/CSUQ.

- The PSSUQ/CSUQ is has been widely used, and is likely to continue being used.

- Its ideal use is when the research setting can tolerate measurement of perceived usability with a 16-item questionnaire and the research benefits from a subscale that measures the perceived quality of information.

- The discovery of correspondence between PSSUQ/CSUQ and SUS scores enables interpretation of PSSUQ/CSUQ means with the Sauro-Lewis curved grading scale, which may lead to additional adoption of the PSSUQ/CSUQ.

- Two areas of research that could contribute to increased adoption of the PSSUQ/CSUQ are (1) additional translation and (2) replication of research investigating correspondence with the SUS.

APPENDIX A:

A Brief Introduction to Standardized Questionnaire Development and Assessment using Classical Test Theory

A questionnaire is a form designed to obtain information from respondents. A common item format for questionnaires is multiple choice, with respondents selecting from a set of alternatives (e.g., "Please select the brand of phone you currently own") or points on a rating scale (e.g., "On a scale of 1 to 5, how satisfied are you with your governor?"). Questionnaires might be designed for a single use or for repeated use in a tracking survey. A standardized questionnaire is one for which there is an established procedure for collecting and presenting the measurement and for which the instrument has undergone psychometric qualification (as described below).

The development of a standardized questionnaire requires substantial effort. After that, however, they are quite economical. Research in usability science (Hornbæk, 2006; Hornbæk & Law, 2007; Sauro & Lewis, 2009) has shown that standardized usability questionnaires have greater reliability than homegrown or ad hoc usability questionnaires. Additional benefits of standardization are (Nunnally, 1978):

- Effective communication among practitioners and researchers
- Enhanced generalizability of findings
- Increased objectivity
- Easier replication

An important aspect of the development of standardized questionnaires is to assess their reliability and validity -- the fundamental elements of psychometric qualification (Nunnally, 1978).

RELIABILITY

The purpose of reliability analysis is to assess the consistency of a measurement. There are a variety of methods (for example, test-retest correlation), but the most common for multi-item questionnaires is coefficient alpha, a measure of internal consistency. Coefficient alpha can range from 0 (completely unreliable) to 1 (perfectly reliable). The typical minimum criterion for acceptable reliability for assessments of sentiment (such as standardized usability questionnaires) is 0.70 (Nunnally, 1978).

VALIDITY

For a standardized measurement to be useful, it must not only be reliable, but it must also measure what it claims to measure -- in other words, it must be valid. The assessment of validity takes a number of forms which typically take place at different times during the development of the instrument. At the beginning of development, the method of item selection drives content validity. There is no easy or universally accepted metric for content validity. Rather, it is assumed as a consequence of starting with an initial pool of items that have rational relationships to the measurement(s) of interest. Those initial items might come from the brainstorming of subject matter experts, from a review of the relevant literature, or both.

Once the questionnaire developers have an initial version of the questionnaire, they begin collecting data -- not only for the questionnaire items but also for other metrics expected to have a relationship with the new metric. Significant correlations between the new metric and the other metrics support claims of concurrent validity.

Construct validity refers to the extent to which the items in a questionnaire group together in the expected pattern. The statistical procedure most often used to assess construct validity is factor analysis. Generally, a factor analysis requires a minimum of five participants per item to ensure stable factor estimates (Nunnally, 1978). There are a number of methods for estimating the number of factors in a set of scores when conducting exploratory analyses, including discontinuity and parallel analysis (Cliff, 1987; Coovert & McNelis, 1988). When previous research (including the research conducted to identify the initial set of items) has established an expected number of factors, there is a shift of focus from exploratory to confirmatory analysis.

ITEM ANALYSIS

Once data has been collected, the next step is to analyze the items to see if it is possible to streamline the questionnaire by deleting the weaker items. One approach to item analysis is to check the alignment of items with the factors computed during factor analysis by examination of the magnitude of the item loadings (similar to correlation coefficients, but with the underlying factors). Items with lower loadings on their factors are candidates for deletion. Another is to examine the correlation between items and related measures hypothesized to measure the same or similar underlying construct or key outcome metrics, keeping items with higher correlations. A third approach is to keep items that discriminate as expected between levels of carefully chosen independent variables. Ideally, these methods would identify the same items as candidates for deletion. If not, then structural considerations (construct validity) generally take priority.

REASSESSMENT OF PSYCHOMETRIC PROPERTIES

After eliminating the weaker items, the next step is to collect additional data to ensure that the questionnaire continues to have acceptable levels of reliability and validity. A second round of item analysis can prompt another iteration of the process, but this is not usually necessary.

DEVELOPMENT OF NORMS

By itself, a score (individual or average) has no meaning. One way to provide meaning is through comparison, either against a benchmark or via comparison of two sets of data (e.g., different products or different user groups). Another is comparison with norms.

Normative data is collected from one or more representative groups who have completed the questionnaire in a specified setting. Comparison with norms allows assessment of how good or bad a score is, within appropriate limits of generalization. With norms there is always a risk that the new sample doesn't match the normative group(s) (Anastasi, 1976), so it is important to understand where the norms came from when using them to interpret new scores.

Few standardized usability questionnaires have strong normative databases. Those that do typically charge license fees for access to those databases (Sauro & Lewis, 2016). An exception is the System Usability Scale (Brooke, 1996). About ten years after its initial publication several researchers compiled a large database from which it was possible to derive a curved grading scale for mean SUS scores which has proven to be of substantial value to usability practitioners working on graphical, Web, and mobile designs (Sauro & Lewis, 2016).

SUMMARY OF STANDARDIZED QUESTIONNAIRE DEVELOPMENT

Figure A.1 summarizes the development method described above. Think about what you're trying to measure (hypothesize construct(s)), develop a set of items, collect data and assess the items, remove weak items and retest, and, finally, develop norms.

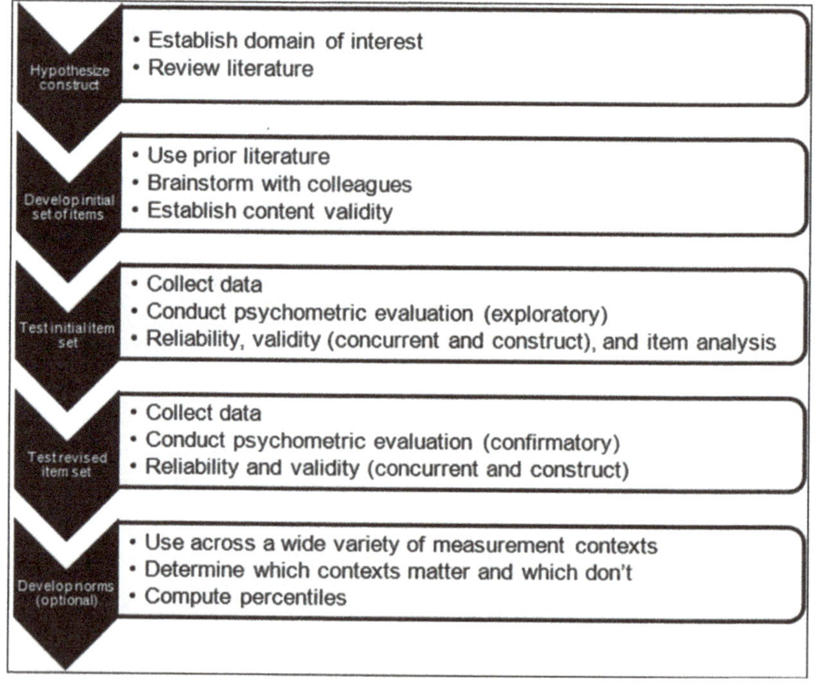

FIGURE A.1: Summary of Standardized Questionnaire Development.

In *Quantifying the User Experience* (Sauro & Lewis, 2016), Jeff Sauro and I provided substantial guidance and numerous quantitative examples of how to estimate sample size requirements. The purpose of this appendix is to cover a few of these methods for some relatively simple cases using data from the chapters in this book. To estimate sample sizes for more complex analyses like ANOVA and multiple regression, we recommended the G*Power tool, available at www.gpower.hhu.de/.

Sample size estimation is intimately related to the computation of confidence intervals. Recall from Chapter 4 that a confidence interval has the form x ± d, where x is a mean and d is the critical difference obtained by multiplying the critical value of t with the standard error of the mean (the standard deviation divided by the square root of the sample size). This means we can use algebra to switch things around to get the formula $n = t^2(s^2)/d^2$, where:

- t is the critical value of t, in other words, the value of t associated with a targeted significance criterion (or analogously, a targeted level of confidence) and a given number of degrees of freedom (df).

- s is the estimated standard deviation.

- d is the critical difference for the experiment, in other words, the smallest difference between the obtained and true value that you need to be able to detect.

Because the critical value of t depends on the expected df, which itself depends on the sample size, it is necessary to iterate to get to the final estimate of the required sample size. Stop iterating when (1) you get the same estimated sample size in two consecutive iterations or (2) when you begin cycling between two estimates.

SAMPLE SIZE ESTIMATION: EXAMPLE 1 – SIMPLE ESTIMATION

Table 4.2 in Chapter 4 showed the results for computing a confidence interval around a mean PSSUQ100 score from a usability study of the CrossPad, with the result 87.54 ± 13.01. For this analysis, n = 6 and s = 12.4.

Suppose it had been important to obtain a more precise estimate of the PSSUQ100, say, one that had a confidence interval width of no more than ±5. Assuming no other changes, especially in the standard deviation, the steps for estimating the required sample size are:

- Start iterations with the z-score in place of t – for 95% confidence (statistical test criterion p < 0.05), this is 1.96.

- Compute the first estimate of n using the equation above – for this data it would be n = $1.96^2(12.4^2)/5^2$ = 23.6. Round this up to 24.

- Run the estimate again, this time with the critical value of t for n-1 (23) df, which is 2.068 in place of z, but keeping everything else the same -- n = $2.068^2(12.4^2)/5^2$ = 26.3. Round this up to 27. Now we know the final value of n will be somewhere between 24 and 27.

- Run the estimate again, this time with the critical value of t for n-1 (26) df of 2.056, keeping everything else the same -- n = $2.056^2(12.4^2)/5^2$ = 25.987, which rounds up to 26.

- Run the estimate again, this time with the critical value of t for n-1 (25) df of 2.0595, keeping everything else the same -- n = $2.0595^2(12.4^2)/5^2$ = 26.088, which rounds up to 27.

- If we continue iterating, the process will cycle between 26 and 27. When this happens, take the average of the two estimates and round up, which in this case would give us n = 27.

So, if it was important to an estimate of the PSSUQ100 from this study within ±5, it would be necessary to collect data from an additional 21 participants.

In the Excel/R companion book to Quantifying the User Experience (Lewis & Sauro, 2016), we provided an R function that performs this iterative computation. Just copy the following text into the R console:

```
# Sample size estimation for one-sample t-test given confidence, power, sd,
critical difference, and 1 vs 2 tailed

# conf is the desired level of confidence expressed as a number between 0 and
1 or between 1 and 100

# e.g., 95% confidence would be .95 or 95

# power is also a number between 0 and 1 or 1 and 100, always one-sided,

# e.g., 50% confidence would be .50 or 50 (with z = 0)

# Uses iteration to estimate required sample size, max of 1000 iterations

#

n.t.onesample.givensd <- function(conf,power,sd,d,tails) {

if (conf > 1) conf <- conf/100

if (power > 1) power <- power/100

var <- sd^2

ncurr <- -1

nprev1 <- -2

nprev2 <- -3

iteration <- 0

if (tails != 1) zconf <- abs(qnorm((1-conf)/2))

if (tails == 1) zconf <- abs(qnorm((1-conf)))

zpower <- abs(qnorm((1-power)))

z <- zconf + zpower

nprev1 <- ceiling((z^2)*var/(d^2))

df <- nprev1 - 1

while ((ncurr != nprev1 ) && (ncurr != nprev2) && (iteration < 1001)) {

iteration <- iteration + 1

nprev2 <- nprev1

nprev1 <- ncurr

if (tails != 1) tconf <- abs(qt((1-conf)/2,df))
```

```
if (tails == 1) tconf <- abs(qt((1-conf),df))

tpower <- abs(qt((1-power),df))

t <- tconf + tpower

ncurr <- ceiling((t^2)*var/(d^2))

df <- ncurr -1

}

cat("\nRESULTS\n\n")

if (ncurr == nprev2 && ncurr < nprev1) cat("No convergence, fluctuating
between:",ncurr,"and",nprev1,"\n")

if (ncurr == nprev2 && ncurr < nprev1) ncurr <- nprev1

cat("Recommended sample size:",ncurr,"\n")

cat("Number of iterations:",iteration,"\n")

if (iteration > 999) cat("WARNING: Over 1000 iterations -- problem
converging \n")

cat("\n")

}
```

This R function, n.t.onesample.givensd, requires five inputs:

- conf: This is the desired level of confidence for intervals and/ or tests of significance, typically set to .95 (95% confidence for intervals, p < 0.05 for tests of significance).

- power: This is where you set the desired power of a test of significance. If you're just estimating a confidence interval around a mean, as in this example, set this to .50 (50% power corresponds to an additional z score of 0, effectively removing power from the calculation).

- sd: This is the standard deviation to use for the estimate, typically a value from a previous study or from a pilot study.

- d: This is the critical value of d, typically based on a researcher's or practitioner's knowledge of the domain or arrived at through discussion with other stakeholders.

- tails: This is where you indicate whether the analysis will be a one- or two-tailed test. The only time it should be one-tailed is when you are testing a mean against a fixed benchmark.

To run this example using the R function, enter:

```
n.t.onesample.givensd(.95, .50, 12.4, 5, 2)
```

This gets the following result in Figure B.1 (which matches the detailed computation above, n = 27):

```
RESULTS

Recommended sample size: 27
Number of iterations: 3
```

FIGURE B.1: Sample Size Estimate for Example 1: R Results.

SAMPLE SIZE ESTIMATION: EXAMPLE 2 – COMPARISON WITH BENCHMARK

Again referring to Table 4.2 in Chapter 4, when we compared that data to a benchmark of 80, we just failed to achieve statistical significance. Assuming everything else stays the same, how large of a sample size would we need to achieve significance?

We can use the n.t.onesample.givensd function to estimate the needed sample size, just changing a few of the parameters. Because this is a test against a benchmark, set "tails" to 1 instead of 2. Set d to the observed difference between the mean and the benchmark (87.54 - 80 = 7.54). We also need to decide what to do about power.

We didn't talk much about the Type II error and power in the brief discussion of tests of significance in Chapter 4 because when you run a test of significance you do so against the criterion you've set against committing a Type I error (p, the likelihood of getting the observed result if there actually is no difference). When you set power to 0.50 when computing the sample size requirement for a test of significance, you're setting the criterion for making a Type II error to 0.5 (remember that the Type II error is the likelihood that you will fail to reject the null hypothesis when there really is a difference). Because that criterion is equal to 1 - power, you can "buy" insurance against making a Type II error by increasing the power of the test. A common goal for power when planning a study is

80% (reducing the probability of a Type II error to 0.20), but note that the price you pay for that insurance is an increase in the required sample size.

Let's see what happens if we compute the sample size requirement twice, once with power set to 50% and once with it set to 80%, using the following commands (with results shown in Figure B.2):

```
n.t.onesample.givensd(.95, .50, 12.4, 7.54, 1)

n.t.onesample.givensd(.95, .80, 12.4, 7.54, 1)
```

```
> n.t.onesample.givensd(.95, .50, 12.4, 7.54, 1)

RESULTS

Recommended sample size: 10
Number of iterations: 2

> n.t.onesample.givensd(.95, .80, 12.4, 7.54, 1)

RESULTS

Recommended sample size: 19
Number of iterations: 2
```

FIGURE B.2: Sample Size Estimates for Example 2: R Results.

If you're willing to accept the risk of a Type II error of 0.5, then you need a total of 10 participants, four more than the six you already have. If you want to reduce the Type II error criterion to 0.2, you'll need a total of 19 participants (13 more than the six you already have).

SAMPLE SIZE ESTIMATION: EXAMPLE 3 – WITHIN-SUBJECTS (DEPENDENT) COMPARISON

Table 4.8 in Chapter 4 had data from four participants who had been in a usability study performing tasks with two personal organizers as part of the Simon project. Even though there was a difference of just over 20 PSSUQ100 points between the two personal organizers, the difference was not statistically significant. Suppose this had been a pilot study to get preliminary estimates of the mean and standard deviation of the difference … what sample size would be required to indicate a statistically significant difference assuming no other changes? What would the estimate be for 50% power, and what would it be for 80% power?

This is another situation in which we are assessing one set of numbers, in this case a set of difference scores where the mean difference was just over 20, the standard deviation of the difference scores was 33.06, and it's a two-tailed test.

```
n.t.onesample.givensd(.95, .50, 33.06, 20, 2)

n.t.onesample.givensd(.95, .80, 33.06, 20, 2)
```

As shown in Figure B.3, if you're willing to risk a Type II error of 0.5, you'll need a total of 13 participants (nine more than the four you already have). For a Type II error risk of 0.2, you'll need a total of 24 participants.

```
> n.t.onesample.givensd(.95, .50, 33.06, 20, 2)

RESULTS

Recommended sample size: 13
Number of iterations: 3

> n.t.onesample.givensd(.95, .80, 33.06, 20, 2)

RESULTS

Recommended sample size: 24
Number of iterations: 2
```

FIGURE B.3: Sample Size Estimates for Example 3: R Results.

SAMPLE SIZE ESTIMATION: EXAMPLE 4 – BETWEEN-SUBJECTS (INDEPENDENT) COMPARISON

Things are a little different for this type of comparison because there are two sets rather than one set of data, each with its own mean and standard deviation. The iterative procedure is similar to the one laid out at the beginning of this appendix, but it's a bit more complex. On the next page is an R function that handles the additional complexity, with the simplifying assumption that the two distributions have equal variances (if that is not a reasonable assumption for your data, use G*Power to estimate the required sample size).

Referring back to Tables 4.6 and 4.7, the test of significance comparing the means from these two VUI studies was not significant. The means were pretty close, differing by just 2.8 PSSUQ100 points. The standard deviation in the first set of data was 14.36, and in the second was 6.85. To average standard deviations, you need to square them to convert them to variances, average the variances, then take the square root of that to get the average standard deviation which, for these data, is about 11.

To run the sample size estimating function on the next page, copy it into the R console, then run the following two commands, one setting the Type II error risk at 0.5 and the other at 0.8.

```
n.t.twosample.givenequalsd(.95, .50, 11, 2.8, 2)
```

```
n.t.twosample.givenequalsd(.95, .80, 11, 2.8, 2)
```

The results are in Figure B.4. Note that the sample size estimate is for one group, but there are two groups in this type of study, so the sample size requirement is the total for two groups. For these data, if you're willing to set the Type II error to 0.5, you would still need a total sample size of 240 to be able to claim significance for a difference as small as 2.8 points on the 0-100-point PSSUQ100 scale. If you wanted the extra protection of 80% power (Type II error set to 0.2), you'd need 488 participants. For most industrial UX work, if you need sample sizes that large to show that a difference is statistically significant, you would probably conclude that for all practical purposes the groups have the same mean.

```
# Sample size estimation for two-sample t-test given confidence, power, sd,
critical difference, and 1 vs 2 tailed

# conf is the desired level of confidence expressed as a number between 0 and
1 or between 1 and 100

# e.g., 95% confidence would be .95 or 95

# power is also a number between 0 and 1 or 1 and 100, always one-sided,

# e.g., 50% confidence would be .50 or 50 (with z = 0)

# Uses iteration to estimate required sample size, max of 1000 iterations

#

n.t.twosample.givenequalsd <- function(conf,power,sd,d,tails) {

if (conf > 1) conf <- conf/100
```

```r
if (power > 1) power <- power/100
var <- sd^2
ncurr <- -1
nprev1 <- -2
nprev2 <- -3
iteration <- 0
if (tails != 1) zconf <- abs(qnorm((1-conf)/2))
if (tails == 1) zconf <- abs(qnorm((1-conf)))
zpower <- abs(qnorm((1-power)))
z <- zconf + zpower
nprev1 <- ceiling(2*(z^2)*var/(d^2))
df <- 2*(nprev1 - 1)
while ((ncurr != nprev1 ) && (ncurr != nprev2) && (iteration < 1001)) {
iteration <- iteration + 1
nprev2 <- nprev1
nprev1 <- ncurr
if (tails != 1) tconf <- abs(qt((1-conf)/2,df))
if (tails == 1) tconf <- abs(qt((1-conf),df))
tpower <- abs(qt((1-power),df))
t <- tconf + tpower
ncurr <- ceiling(2*(t^2)*var/(d^2))
df <- 2*(ncurr - 1)
}
cat("\nRESULTS\n\n")
if (ncurr == nprev2 && ncurr < nprev1) cat("No convergence, fluctuating
between:",ncurr,"and",nprev1,"\n")
if (ncurr == nprev2 && ncurr < nprev1) ncurr <- nprev1
cat("Recommended sample size per group:",ncurr,"\n")
cat("Recommended total sample size:",2*ncurr,"\n")
cat("Number of iterations:",iteration,"\n")
```

if (iteration > 999) cat("WARNING: Over 1000 iterations -- problem converging \n")

cat("\n")

}

```
> n.t.twosample.givenequalsd(.95,  .50,  11,  2.8,  2)

RESULTS

Recommended sample size per group: 120
Recommended total sample size: 240
Number of iterations: 2

> n.t.twosample.givenequalsd(.95,  .80,  11,  2.8,  2)

RESULTS

Recommended sample size per group: 244
Recommended total sample size: 488
Number of iterations: 2
```

FIGURE B.4: Sample Size Estimates for Example 4: R Results.

Anastasi, A. (1976). *Psychological testing*. New York, NY: Macmillan.

Bagheri, E., & Ghorbani, A. A. (2009). A belief-theoretic framework for the collaborative development and integration of para-consistent models. *Journal of Systems and Software, 82*, 707–729.

Bangor, A., Kortum, P. T., & Miller, J. T. (2008). An empirical evaluation of the System Usability Scale. *International Journal of Human–Computer Interaction, 24*, 574–594.

Bangor, A., Kortum, P. T., & Miller, J. T. (2009). Determining what individual SUS scores mean: Adding an adjective rating scale. *Journal of Usability Studies, 4(3)*, 114–123.

Barnette, J. J. (2000). Effects of stem and Likert response option reversals on survey internal consistency: If you feel the need, there is a better alternative to using those negatively worded stems. *Educational and Psychological Measurement, 60*, 361–370.

Baumgartner, H., & Steenkamp, J. B. E. M. (2001). Response styles in marketing research: A cross-national investigation. *Journal of Marketing Research, 38*, 143–156.

Benedek, J., & Miner, T. (2002). Measuring desirability: New methods for evaluating desirability in a usability lab setting. Paper presented at the *Usability Professionals Association Annual Conference*. Orlando, FL: UPA.

Benjamini, Y., & Yekutieli, D. (2001). The control of the false discovery rate in multiple testing under dependency. *The Annals of Statistics, 29(4)*, 1165-1188.

Berkman, M. I., & Karahoca, D. (2016). Re-assessing the usability metric for user experience (UMUX) scale. *Journal of Usability Studies, 11(3)*, 89–109.

Brooke, J. (1996). SUS: A "quick and dirty" usability scale. In P. Jordan, B. Thomas, & B. Weerdmeester (Eds.), *Usability Evaluation in Industry* (pp. 189-194). London, UK: Taylor & Francis.

Brooke, J. (2013). SUS: A retrospective. *Journal of Usability Studies, 8(2)*, 29-40.

Cheung, G.W., & Rensvold, R. B. (2000). Assessing extreme and acquiescence response sets in cross-cultural research using structural equations modeling. *Journal of Cross-Cultural Psychology, 31*, 187–212.

Chin, J. P., Diehl, V. A., & Norman, K. L. (1988). Development of an instrument measuring user satisfaction of the human-computer interface. In *Proceedings of CHI 1988* (pp. 213-218). Washington, DC: ACM.

Chow, M., & Chan, L., (2010). Development and evaluation of a compartmental picture archiving and communications system model for integration and visualization of multidisciplinary biomedical data to facilitate student learning health clinic. *Computers & Education, 54*, 733–741.

Clarke, I. (2001). Extreme response style in cross-cultural research. *International Marketing Review, 18*, 301–324.

Cliff, N. (1987). *Analyzing multivariate data.* San Diego, CA: Harcourt Brace Jovanovich.

Christophersen, R., & Konradt, U. (2011). Reliability, validity, and sensitivity of a single-item measure of online store usability. *International Journal of Human–Computer Studies, 69*, 269–280.

Coovert, M. D., & McNelis, K. (1988). Determining the number of common factors in factor analysis: A review and program. *Educational and Psychological Measurement, 48*, 687-693.

Davis, D. (1989). Perceived usefulness, perceived ease of use, and user acceptance of information technology. *MIS Quarterly, 13(3)*, 319-339.

Erdinç, O., & Lewis, J. R. (2013). Psychometric evaluation of the T-CSUQ: The Turkish version of the Computer System Usability Questionnaire. *International Journal of Human-Computer Interaction, 29(5)*, 319-326.

Finstad, K. (2010). The usability metric for user experience. *Interacting with Computers, 22(5)*, 323–327.

Frias-Martinez, E., Chen, S.Y., & Liu, X. (2009). Evaluation of a personalized digital library based on cognitive styles: Adaptivity vs. adaptability. *International Journal of Information Management, 29*, 48–56.

Hornbæk, K. (2006). Current practice in measuring usability: Challenges to usability studies and research. *International Journal of Human-Computer Studies, 64(2)*, 79–102.

Hornbæk, K., & Law, E.L. (2007). Meta-analysis of correlations among usability measures. In *Proceedings of CHI 2007* (pp. 617-626). San Jose, CA: ACM.

Ibrahim, A. M. (2001). Differential responding to positive and negative items: The case of a negative item in a questionnaire for course and faculty evaluation. *Psychological Reports, 88*, 497–500.

ISO, 1998. *Ergonomic requirements for office work with visual display terminals (VDTs), Part 11, Guidance on usability (ISO 9241-11:1998E).* Geneva, Switzerland: Author.

Kartakis, S., & Stephanidis, C. (2010). A design-and-play approach to accessible user interface development in Ambient Intelligence environments. *Computers in Industry, 61*, 318–328.

Kirakowski, J., & Corbett, M. (1993). SUMI: The Software Usability Measurement Inventory. *British Journal of Educational Psychology, 24*, 210-212.

Kirakowski, J., & Dillon, A. (1988). *The Computer User Satisfaction Inventory (CUSI): Manual and scoring key.* Cork, Ireland: Human Factors Research Group, University College of Cork.

Kortum, P., & Bangor, A. (2013). Usability ratings for everyday products measured with the System Usability Scale. *International Journal of Human-Computer Interaction, 29*, 67–76.

Kortum, P., & Sorber, M. (2015). Measuring the usability of mobile applications for phones and tablets. *International Journal of Human-Computer Interaction, 31(8)*, 518–529.

Lewis, J. R. (1990). *Psychometric evaluation of a post-study system usability questionnaire: The PSSUQ* (Tech. Report 54.535). Boca Raton, FL: International Business Machines Corp.

Lewis, J. R. (1992). Psychometric evaluation of the Post-Study System Usability Questionnaire: the PSSUQ. In *Proceedings of the Human Factors Society 36th Annual Meeting* (pp. 1259-1263), Santa Monica, CA: Human Factors Society.

Lewis, J. R. (1995). IBM computer usability satisfaction questionnaires: Psychometric evaluation and instructions for use. *International Journal of Human-Computer Interaction, 7*, 57–78.

Lewis, J. R. (1996). Reaping the benefits of modern usability evaluation: The Simon story. In G. Salvendy & A. Ozok (Eds.), *Advances in applied ergonomics: Proceedings of the 1st International Conference on Applied Ergonomics—ICAE '96* (pp. 752–757). Istanbul, Turkey: USA Publishing.

Lewis, J. R. (1999). Effect of error correction strategy on speech dictation throughput. In *Proceedings of the Human Factors and Ergonomics Society 43rd Annual Meeting* (pp. 457-461). Santa Monica, CA: HFES.

Lewis, J. R. (2001). *The accuracy wars: Journalists' estimates of continuous speech product dictation accuracy from 1997-1999* (IBM Tech. Report 29.3465). West Palm Beach, FL: IBM Corp.

Lewis, J. R. (2002). Psychometric evaluation of the PSSUQ using data from five years of usability studies. *International Journal of Human-Computer Interaction, 14*, 463-488.

Lewis, J. R. (2004). Selection accuracy with pen selection slots. In *Proceedings of the Human Factors and Ergonomics Society 48th Annual Meeting* (pp. 783-787). Santa Monica, CA: HFES.

Lewis, J. R. (2012). Usability testing. In G. Salvendy (Ed.), *Handbook of Human Factors and Ergonomics, 4th ed.* (pp. 1267-1312). New York, NY: John Wiley, New York, NY.

Lewis, J. R. (2014). Usability: Lessons learned . . . and yet to be learned. *International Journal of Human-Computer Interaction, 30*, 663-684.

Lewis, J. R. (2018a). Is the report of the death of the construct of usability an exaggeration? *Journal of Usability Studies, 14(1)*, 1-7.

Lewis, J. R. (2018b). Measuring perceived usability: The CSUQ, SUS, and UMUX. *International Journal of Human-Computer Interaction, 34(12)*, 1148-1156.

Lewis, J. R. (2018c). Measuring perceived usability: SUS, UMUX, and CSUQ ratings for four everyday products. DOI: 10.1080/10447318.2018.1533152

Lewis, J. R. (2018d). The System Usability Scale: Past, present, and future. *International Journal of Human-Computer Interaction, 34(7)*, 577-590.

Lewis, J. R. (In press). Comparison of four TAM item formats: Effect of response option labels and order. To appear in the *Journal of Usability Studies*.

Lewis, J. R., Henry, S. C., & Mack, R. L. (1990). Integrated office software benchmarks: A case study. In D. Diaper et al. (Ed.), *Proceedings of the 3rd IFIP Conference on Human-Computer Interaction, INTERACT '90* (pp. 337-343). Cambridge, UK: Elsevier Science.

Lewis, J. R., & Sauro, J. (2016). *Excel and R Companion to the 2nd Edition of Quantifying the User Experience*. Denver, CO: Create Space Publishing.

Lewis, J. R., Utesch, B. S., & Maher, D. E. (2013, April). UMUX-LITE: When there's no time for the SUS. In *Proceedings of the SIGCHI Conference on Human Factors in Computing Systems* (pp. 2099–2102). New York, NY: ACM.

MacDorman, K. F., Whalen, T. J., Ho, C., & Patel, H. (2011). An improved usability measure based on novice and expert performance. *International Journal of Human–Computer Interaction, 27*, 280–302.

McNamara, N., & Kirakowski, J. (2011). Measuring user-satisfaction with electronic consumer products: The Consumer Products Questionnaire. *International Journal of Human–Computer Studies, 69*, 375–386.

Nielsen, J., & Mack, R. L. (1994). *Usability inspection methods*. New York, NY: John Wiley.

Nunnally, J. C. (1978). *Psychometric theory*. New York, NY: McGraw-Hill.

Pereira, J. A., Quach, S., Hamid, J. S., Heidebrecht, C. L., Quan, S. D., Nassif, J., . . . Kwong, J. C. (2012). Exploring the feasibility of integrating barcode scanning technology into vaccine inventory recording in seasonal influenza vaccination clinics. *Vaccine, 30*, 794–802.

Saleem, J. J., Haggstrom, D. A., Militello, L. G., Flanagan, M., Kiess, C. L., Arbuckle, N., & Doebbling, B. N. (2011). Redesign of a computerized clinical reminder for colorectal cancer screening: A human computer interaction evaluation. *BMC Medical Informatics and Decision Making, 11*, 1–11.

Sauro, J. (2011). *A practical guide to the System Usability Scale (SUS): Background, benchmarks & best practices*. Denver, CO: Measuring Usability LLC.

Sauro, J. (2018). *Benchmarking the user experience*. Denver, CO: MeasuringU Press.

Sauro, J., & Lewis, J. R. (2009). Correlations among prototypical usability metrics: Evidence for the construct of usability. In *Proceedings of CHI 2009* (pp. 1609-1618). Boston, MA: Association for Computing Machinery.

Sauro, J., & Lewis, J. R. (2011). When designing usability questionnaires, does it hurt to be positive? In *Proceedings of CHI 2011* (pp. 2215-2223). Vancouver, Canada: ACM.

Sauro, J., & Lewis, J. R. (2016). *Quantifying the user experience: Practical statistics for user research (2ⁿᵈ ed.)*. Cambridge, MA: Morgan Kaufmann.

Savidis, A., Grammenos, D., & Stephanidis, C. (2006). Developing inclusive e-learning systems. *Universal Access in the Information Society, 5*, 51–72.

Searles, D. (1978). PSI burn: A study of physiological deterioration in parapsychological experimentation. *Omni Magazine, 1(3)*, 108-110.

Travis, D. (2008). Measuring satisfaction: Beyond the usability questionnaire. Available from: www.userfocus.co.uk/articles/satisfaction.html

Tullis, T. S., & Albert, B. (2008). *Measuring the user experience: Collecting, analyzing, and presenting usability metrics*. Burlington, MA: Morgan Kaufmann.

Tullis, T. S., & Stetson, J. N. (2004). *A comparison of questionnaires for assessing website usability*. Paper presented at the Usability Professionals Association Annual Conference. UPA, Minneapolis, MN. Available also at https://www.researchgate.net/publication/228609327_A_Comparison_of_Questionnaires_for_Assessing_Website_Usability (accessed September 13, 2017).

van de Vijver, F. J. R., & Leung, K. (2001). Personality in cultural context: Methodological issues. *Journal of Personality, 69*, 1007–1031.

van Lammeren, R., Houtkamp, J., Colijn, S., Hilferink, M., & Bouwman, A. (2010). Affective appraisal of 3D land use visualization. *Computers, Environment and Urban Systems, 34*, 465–475.

Whiteside, J., Bennett, J., & Holzblatt, K. (1988). Usability engineering: Our experience and evolution. In M. Helander (Ed.), *Handbook of Human-Computer Interaction* (pp. 791-817). Amsterdam, Netherlands: North-Holland.

www.ingramcontent.com/pod-product-compliance
Lightning Source LLC
Chambersburg PA
CBHW041219050726
47599CB00001B/7